Short Films in Language Teaching

SELT STUDIES IN ENGLISH LANGUAGE TEACHING

Augsburger Studien zur Englischdidaktik

Edited by Engelbert Thaler (Augsburg)

Editorial Board:
Sabine Doff (Bremen), Michaela Sambanis (Berlin), Daniela Elsner (Frankfurt am Main), Carola Surkamp (Göttingen), Christiane Lütge (München), Petra Kirchhoff (Regensburg)

Volume 2

Engelbert Thaler (ed.)

Short Films in Language Teaching

narr\f
ranck
e\atte
mpto

Bibliografische Information der Deutschen Nationalbibliothek
Die Deutsche Nationalbibliothek verzeichnet diese Publikation in der Deutschen
Nationalbibliografie; detaillierte bibliografische Daten sind im Internet über http://dnb.
dnb.de abrufbar.

© 2017 · Narr Francke Attempto Verlag GmbH + Co. KG
Dischingerweg 5 · D-72070 Tübingen

Das Werk einschließlich aller seiner Teile ist urheberrechtlich geschützt. Jede Verwertung außerhalb der engen Grenzen des Urheberrechtsgesetzes ist ohne Zustimmung des Verlages unzulässig und strafbar. Das gilt insbesondere für Vervielfältigungen, Übersetzungen, Mikroverfilmungen und die Einspeicherung und Verarbeitung in elektronischen Systemen.

Gedruckt auf säurefreiem und alterungsbeständigem Werkdruckpapier.
Internet: www.narr.de
E-Mail: info@narr.de

Printed in Germany
ISSN 2367-3826
ISBN 978-3-8233-8098-6

Contents

Introduction 7

A. Theory

Engelbert Thaler
Short Films in English Language Teaching 13

Klaus Maiwald
Goose Bumps – How the Language of Film Enters into
Language Teaching with Films 27

Annika McPherson
Afrofuturist Interventions into the Postcolonial:
Wanuri Kahiu's *Pumzi* 37

B. Methodology

Gabriele Blell
Viral Videos in the EFL Classroom 51

Christiane Lütge
Amazing Short Animation: »Must See / Teach«
Films for the EFL Classroom 65

Matthias Hutz
Exposing Learners to Authentic Language in
Short Video Clips in the EFL Classroom 73

Christoph Werth
Dumb Ways to Die – a Morbid But Fun Way to
Learn with a *Shorty* 87

Genia Markova, Jana Pessozki
Father and Daughter – An Animation Film for
All Foreign Languages 101

C. Lessons

Lena Heinze
New Silent Short Films 111

Anja Boneberger, Zeynep Direk, Dominik Eberts, Demet Gürsoy
Commercials 129

Susanne Klohn
Animated Shorts 139

Susanne Neumann
Infrographic Films 149

Lea Mittelstädt, Maria Sachsinger, Linda Ringwald
Social Shorts 161

Lea Mittelstädt, Maria Sachsinger, Linda Ringwald
Viral Shorts 165

Stefanie Rödel
Documentaries 173

Angelika Pfeil
Weather Forecasts 179

Contributors 189

Introduction

Why is a short film a perfect medium for teaching English as a foreign language? The simple though tautological answer is … because it is short, and it is a film. »If it moves, they will watch it« (Andy Warhol).

Looking back at the history of film, one realizes that the very first films shown to the public in 1894 were very short films presenting celebrities, current affairs and everyday life scenes. With the advent of feature-length films, due to recording and editing advances, commercial cinema gradually discarded short films. Yet technological progress in the fields of digital video, mobile devices, editing tools, and video sharing websites, has led to a renaissance of the short film (Donaghy 2015: 24). The internet turns out to match producers and consumers of short films in a marvellous way: The first can post their films online with no expenditure and reach millions of viewers; the latter can indulge in short bursts of entertainment anywhere and anytime.

This omnipresence should not exclude the classroom. Donaghy (2015: 24f.) propounds several convincing arguments for exploiting the ascent of the short film in TEFL. Short films …

- can be easily integrated into the classroom, in contrast to feature films,
- tell a whole narrative in a short period of time, allowing teachers to focus on narrative structure and character development,
- are often open to different levels of interpretation,
- can captivate, surprise, inspire and provoke learners as they are usually unfamiliar to them,
- often have little dialogue, enabling intensive filmic experiences,
- are excellent prompts for oral and written communication,
- can promote film literacy better than long formats as they are less intimidating.

For all these reasons, this book is dedicated to the use of short films in TEFL. As all edited volumes in the SELT (Studies in English Language Teaching) series, it follows a **triple aim**:

a. Linking TEFL with related academic disciplines
b. Balancing TEFL research and classroom practice
c. Combining theory, methodology and exemplary lessons

This triple aim is reflected in the **three-part structure** of this volume. In Part A (Theory), the topic of short films is investigated from the perspectives of three academic disciplines, i.e. from the viewpoints of TEFL, film studies and cultural studies. Part B (Methodology) assembles five contributions on selected films, media and techniques. Eight concrete lesson plans can be found in Part C (Classroom). These lessons were designed by lecturer (editor) and students in university courses, then conducted and assessed by teachers at German schools, and finally revised by the editor. Each of these eight chapters is divided into genre (brief background information on the film type), procedure (source, synopsis, competences, topics, level, time, phases of the lesson), materials (texts, worksheets, board sketches), solutions (expected answers), and bibliography.

Part A is introduced by the **TEFL perspective**. **Engelbert Thaler** attempts to answer what is meant by short films, why they should be used in the TEFL classroom, where teachers can find suitable material, what subgenres can be distinguished, what criteria of selection may be applied, what objectives can be determined, and how short films can actually be exploited in language classes. The theoretical argumentation is supported by the description and analysis of several film examples.

The perspective of **film studies** is adopted by **Klaus Maiwald**. First he outlines didactic reasons and directions of working with (short) films. Then he takes a closer look at the innertextual and intertextual qualities of a particular short film (Goose Bumps / *Gänsehaut*), showing how the language of film, its formal means and aesthetic techniques, is integral to language learning with film. He concludes by claiming that while film analysis is no end in itself, it is required in defining and fulfilling language oriented tasks.

Annika McPherson adopts the perspective of **cultural studies**. She analyzes the award-winning 2009 short film *Pumzi* (›Breath‹ in Swahili). Building upon different readings of the film, her contribution highlights the film's Afrofuturist dimension. It draws on cultural studies and postcolonial studies frameworks in order to show how broader questions of agency surrounding cultural power and cultural politics can be addressed through the analysis and discussion of Pumzi in educational contexts.

Part B is introduced by **Gabriele Blell**. She treats the teaching potential of **viral videos** in school on a theoretical, a methodological and a practical level. The outstanding *Yes, We Can* by Will.I.Am (2008) is used as an illustration, and a possible teaching scenario initiated by a complex task is offered.

Christiane Lütge recommends short **animation films**. She explores the potential of this genre, suggests a list of »must-see / teach« films, and encourages teachers to have learners produce their own animated videos.

Matthias Hutz exposes his learners to real-life language and interaction through shorties. After examining the difficulties of authentic language, he proposes several ideas how students can cope with **authenticity**.

Christoph Werth uses the children's *Schadenfreude* to instigate learning processes concerning vocabulary and grammar as well as to make them reflect their attitudes towards a topic as serious as death and dying. However, he adopts a humorous approach to this topic by working with the short movie ***Dumb Ways to Die***.

Genia Markova and **Jana Pessozki** recommend the short **silent animation film** ***Father and Daughter***, which tells a very special story of a loss. Artful and elaborate, using only music and pictures to convey the message, this wonderful film can promote visual comprehension, writing and film analysis.

Part C comprises eight contributions, which demonstrate how certain subgenres of short films can be employed in the English language classroom:

- **New silent short films** are recommended by **Lena Heinze**, who suggests inspiring lesson ideas for the film *Gift*. While watching, one wonders whether the family has really adopted a girl ... or is it a ...?
- What genre has got »shock, beauty, atmosphere, glamour, drama, comedy, all in the space of 15–30 seconds?« (Sherman) Right, it's the **commercial**. **Anja Boneberger, Zeynep Direk, Dominik Eberts** and **Demet Gürsoy** present two examples, i.e. a car commercial with the famous actor Pierce Brosnan, and a MetLife clip, in which a young girl exposes her father to be a liar.
- Why not take a closer look at **animated shorts**? **Susanne Klohn** introduces us to a young boy, who gets a present from his mother, but there's something wrong with the puppy: One of its legs is missing.
- **Infographic films** can transform complex information into graphics, which are both easy to grasp and visually appealing. Hence **Susanne Neumann** makes us familiar with the fast food industry and a study of Twitter users.
- »How do you turn a life around?« If you are stumped for an answer, watch this thought-provoking example of **social shorts** about First (?) World problems presented by **Lea Mittelstädt, Maria Sachsinger** and **Linda Ringwald**.
- The same ladies convince us that people become unsocial by using social media. Ironically the **viral video** *Look up*, which calls upon us to look up from our mobile phones, has gone viral.
- A long-established yet still vigorous genre is the **documentary**. **Stefanie Rödel** allures us to visit South Africa by revealing »Top 10 amazing facts« about this country.
- Everybody talks about the weather. Taking the phatic function of weather in communication seriously, our meteorologist **Angelika Pfeil** presents **weather forecasts**.

In short, short films can be wonderful media for TEFL classrooms. Due to »their accessibility, brevity, innovation and creativity, short films are the perfect vehicle for using moving images in the language learning classroom – and for promoting both oral *and* written communication« (Donaghy 2015: 25). And the importance of short films is likely to rise as newer, simpler and cheaper forms of creating, distributing and viewing short films are about to develop.

A. Theory

Short Films in English Language Teaching

Engelbert Thaler

»I hate it when my house is so big I need two wireless routers« – this is what a poor black man, standing in front of a tiny, decrepit wooden hut, is complaining about in the short film *First World Problems* (www.viralvideoaward.com/first-world-problems). This viral video, directed by the American Alec Helm (2012), is a tongue-in-cheek jab at complaints that are only voiced by privileged individuals in wealthy countries. Although it lasts only 1:01 minutes, it can be exploited for all the competences asked for in the educational standards (KMK 2012, Fig. 1).

Competences	First World Problems
Functional communicative competences:	
• Listening-viewing	• Recognizing the satirical clash between words and visuals
• Speaking	• Discussing trivial inconveniences
• Reading	• Reading the subtitles
• Writing	• Adding a comment on YouTube
• Mediating	• Transferring statements into L1
• Lexical competence	• Explaining unknown words, e.g. »mint gums«
• Grammatical competence	• Revising passive voice, e.g. »… my leather seats aren't heated …«
• Pronunciation	• Repeating the statements in RP
• Spelling	• Distinguishing between BE and AE, e.g. »neighbours« / »neighbors«
Text and media competence	Investigating the make-up and impact of viral videos

Competences	First World Problems
Intercultural communicative competence	Exploring the chasm between First and Third World
Language awareness	Bringing multilingualism, ESL and lingua franca to mind
Language learning competence	Making students aware of the language learning potential of short film platforms

Fig. 1: *First World Problems* video & educational standards

The following paper attempts to answer what is meant by short films, why they should be used in the TEFL classroom, where teachers can find suitable material, what subgenres can be distinguished, what criteria of selection may be applied, what objectives can be determined, and how short films can actually be exploited in language classes. The theoretical argumentation will be supported by the description and analysis of several film examples, which are described with the help of six criteria: title, type, source, synopsis, features, and learning potential.

1 Term

According to length, films can be divided into long formats, medium formats, and short formats (Thaler 2014, Fig. 2).

Types	Length	Examples
Short formats	1 sec – 20 min	see below
Medium formats	20–45 min	• drama series • sitcoms • soap operas • talk shows • game shows • documentaries • educational films
Long formats	45+ minutes	• feature films • live coverage of (inter)national events

Fig. 2: Film formats

2 Justification

Why should we employ short films in our classrooms? A circular and tautological answer would be because they are short and audiovisual.

Apart from the general benefits of using films in TEFL such as popularity, motivation audio-visual appeal, authenticity, personal relevance and teachers' preferences (Stempleski/Tomalin 2001, Thaler 2007a), short formats exhibit additional didactic assets:

- Time: Compared to long audiovisual formats, e.g. movies, and medium formats, e.g. sitcoms, short films can be comfortably dealt with in a 45-minute lesson including viewing and working phases.
- Repetition: Due to their brevity, double or even triple viewing is possible.
- Focus: Certain details like camera perspective, character development, leitmotif or central message can be studied in detail within a manageable context.
- Flexibility: The three time-saving approaches to presenting films, i.e. segment, sandwich, and appetizer approach, are dispensable as the very short format allows for a simple straight-through mode (cf. Thaler 2014). The working phases may be structured according to the PWP (pre – while – post), GTD (global to detail), TBLL (task-based language learning), 10-step listening-viewing approach, or MVC (7-code music video clip) patterns (Thaler 2012).

All these benefits are not hard to be detected in the famous 40-second Berlitz commercial called *The German Coast Guard* (Fig. 3, also see Thaler 2014).

Title	The German Coast Guard
Type	Commercial
Source	www.youtube.com/watch?v=yR0lWICH3rY
Synopsis	In this hilarious Berlitz commercial, a young German coastguard is being given instructions in his new job by an elderly man. As soon as the experienced man leaves, the trainee receives a distress call from an English boat: »We are sinking!« After a pause the coastguard asks: »What are you sinking (thinking) about?«
Features	• Brevity (40 sec) • Humour • Polyvalence

Learning potential	• Pronunciation: problems with /th/ • Linguistics: minimal pairs »thinking / sinking« • Grammar: present progressive • Mediation: L1-L2 (first part) • Speaking: sources of humour • Lingua franca: sea travel • Intercultural learning: *critical incidents* • Advertising: form, function and impact of a commercial

Fig. 3: *The German Coast Guard*

Moreover, not only media literacy / film literacy, but basically all competence domains and individual sub-competences that are postulated in the educational standards (KMK 2003, KMK 2012) can be fostered with the help of short films:

- Functional communicative competences ► particularly listening-viewing
- Intercultural communicative competence ► culture-specific references
- Text and media competence ► cinematic devices
- Language awareness ► sociolects, regiolects
- Language learning competence ► Extramural English with online platforms

3 Resources

Where can teachers – and learners – find suitable material when they want to make use of short films? The following table provides a few suggestions (Fig. 4).

Film guides	• http://www.filmsite.org • http://www.imdb.com • http://www.filmclub.org • http://filmeducation.org • http://www.eslnotes.com/synopses.html
Learner film sites	• www.english-attack.com • http://learnenglishteens.britishcouncil.org/uk-now/film-uk
Lesson plans	• http://lessonstream.org • http://viralelt.wordpress.com

Film scripts	• http://www.dailyscript.com • http://www.script-o-rama.com
Animated movie makers	• http://goanimate.com • http://www.zimmertwins.com
Subtitling and revoicing	• http://www.grapheine.com/bombaytv • http://clipflair.net
Kieran Donaghy	• http://filminaction.com • http://film-english.com

Fig. 4: TEFL resources

4 Types

Short films may be classified according to length (one-second films, one-minute films, short shorts, etc.), genre (comedy, drama, documentary, horror, romance, sci-fi, thriller, etc.), topic (animals, coming-of-age, dance, superhero, etc.), or artistic claim (Heinrich 1997, Monaco 2009, Keddie 2014). Although in the era of post-modern hybridity, the boundaries between ad and art, or trash and treasure, are blurred, short films with rather aesthetic ambitions can be detected. These art shorts are also awarded prizes at international short film festivals such as the Tampere International Short Film Festival or the New York Short Film Festival. An example well worth seeing is *Father and Daughter* (2000), a multi-award winning 8-minute animated film directed by Michael Dudok de Wit, which completely forgoes any dialogues (see Pessozki in this volume).

Apart from art shorts, one can find several traditional types whose artistic ambitions are limited (Keddie 2014, Thaler 2014, 2000):

- music videos
- sketches / skits
- trailers
- TV news
- weather forecasts
- interviews
- commercials

Brave new digital world has recently given birth to further innovative short film genres (Donaghy 2015: 25 ff., Fig. 5).

New types of short films

1. Branded Shorts

short films created for a company / brand ▶ fusion between advertising and entertainment, innovative narratives, high production standards

2. Social Shorts

dealing with social themes such as poverty, homelessness, discrimination ▶ social awareness, emotional involvement, dramatic appeal

3. Literal Music Videos

music videos in which the original lyrics have been replaced by lines that depict the content of the visuals ▶ parody, wit, musical appeal, cinematic analysis (!), working with lyrics (vocabulary)

4. Infographic Films

animated representations of information, data, knowledge ▶ full of facts, appealing to visual learners

5. Viral Shorts
short films that become very popular through being shared rapidly and widely on the Internet ▶ funny, strange, powerful, discussing the impact

6. Animated Lectures

lectures created by pairing leading experts in a field with talented animators ▶ intellectual challenge, reduction of complexity by combining audio, text and attractive animation, presenting world-renowned experts (example: RSA ANIMATE: Changing Education Paradigms, talk given at the RSA by Sir Ken Robinson, www.youtube.com/watch?v=zDZFcDGpL4U)

7. Split-screen Shorts

films with a visible division of the screen into two halves, with different moving images in each half ▶ discussing similarities and differences between the two screens

8. Response Films

shorts which criticise or parody the content and message of another film (viral or branded shorts), often in a humorous or hard-hitting manner ▶ criticism of the original, promoting critical thinking, learners producing their own film as a reaction to a manipulative clip

9. New Silent Short Films

shorts without any dialogue, produced recently ▶ lack of text, suitable for various proficiency levels

10. Mash-ups

montages or combinations of two or more already existing films ▶ promoting genre competence, producing one's own mash-ups

Fig. 5: New short film genres

An example of a viral short, which treats a current problem in an illuminating yet non-obtrusive manner, is delineated in Fig. 6.

Title	*I Forgot My Phone*
Type	Viral short
Source	www.youtube.com/watch?v=OINa46HeWg8
Synopsis	The two-minute film, a hyper-real vision of everyday life, shows various social situations, in which groups of people are utterly engrossed by their phones instead of the world around them. Whether it is taking in a spectacular view, holding a conversation with friends, innocently enjoying a swing, or lying in bed with a partner, the phone takes precedence over real life. This satirical jab at society's obsession with their mobile phones highlights our inability to enjoy the here and now (mindfulness).
Features	• Huge popularity • Current social problem • Language (words) not relevant
Learning potential	• First viewing: vision off approach • Discussing excessive mobile use • Reading / responding to YouTube comments

Fig. 6: *I Forgot My Phone*

5 Selection

The preference for a certain film genre may be one guideline when having to choose an appropriate film for one's class. Further criteria of selection are the following (Thaler 2017a):

- linguistic complexity
- audio-visual comprehensibility
- language quantity
- didactic exploitability
- pedagogic concerns
- topical relevance
- length
- sound-vision relation
- aesthetic quality

An example that fulfils quite a lot of these criteria is outlined in Fig. 7.

Title	*Splitscreen: A Love Story*
Type	Split-screen story
Source	https://vimeo.com/25451551
Synopsis	Two lovebirds wake up on opposite sides of the world (New York, Paris), and start parallel journeys to meet each other. The story is told simultaneously through the eyes of the two characters, and each shot is meticulously matched to its transatlantic counterpart, e.g. a truck in Paris seamlessly becomes a New York City taxi.
Features	• Split screen • Paris and New York • No text / dialogues • Winner of Nokia shorts competition 2011 • Completely shot on Nokia N8 mobile phone
Learning potential	• Usable in various languages • Analysis of cinematic devices • Description, retelling, discussion

Fig. 7: *Splitscreen: A Love Story*

6 Objectives

In analogy to the model of film literacy (Thaler 2014), one can postulate three domains and three skills for short films as well (Fig. 8).

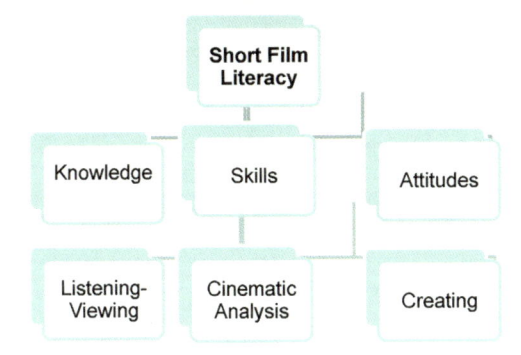

Fig. 8: Short Film Literacy

Short films are predestined for cinematic analysis, so Fig. 9 outlines a literal music video which abounds in film devices.

Title	*Total Eclipse of the Heart*
Type	Literal music video
Source	https://www.youtube.com/watch?v=fsgWUq0fdKk
Synopsis	A literal music video is a parody of an official music video clip in which the lyrics have been replaced with lyrics that describe the visuals in the video – so you really hear what you see in this spoof on Bonnie Tyler's classic music video of the 80s, e.g. *(Pan the room) Random use of candles, empty bottles, and cloth, and can you see me through this fan? (Slo-mo dove) Creepy doll, a window, and what looks like a bathrobe. Then, a dim-lit shot of dangling balls. (Metaphor?)* ...
Features	• Parody and humour • Deconstructing a cult song / video • Cinematographic techniques
Learning potential	• Comparing original and parody • Film analysis (cinematic devices) • Lexical work and ICC • Creative production of one's own literal music video

Fig. 9: *Total Eclipse of the Heart*

7 Methodology

When structuring a teaching unit on short films, one can resort to the well-known lesson planning patterns (Thaler 2012, 2007b):

- PPP (presentation, practice, production)
- PWP (pre-while-post)
- GtD (global-to-detail)
- TBLL (Task-based Language Learning)
- Music Video Approach (3 codes, 7 combinations)

In order to focus on listening-viewing or / and cinematic analysis, the 10-step approach can be recommended (Thaler 2014, Fig. 10).

Step	Phase	Content / Functions
1	Lead-in	- Introducing the situation: who, what ... - Justifying the need to watch
2	Prep work	- Key phrases - Intercultural background
3	1st purpose	- Intention (global understanding) - Tasks
4	1st viewing	Whole film
5	Global comprehension	- Students' answers
6	2nd purpose	- Intention (detailed understanding) - Tasks
7	2nd viewing	Film
8	Detailed comprehension	Students' answers
9	(optional: 3rd viewing)	- Focusing task - Part of film - Discussion
10	Wrap-up	- Follow-up activities - Analysis - Discussion - Transfer

Fig. 10: 10-step approach to listening-viewing

This 10-step approach can be exemplified with the hilarious black humour skit *Fatal Beatings* (www.youtube.com/watch?v=fZMoB6ms2mE), in which a meeting between a strict headmaster (Rowan Atkinson) and a worried student's father rapidly goes downhill after the headmaster mentions casually that he has beaten his son to death (Fig. 11).

Step	Phase	Content
1	Lead-in	T activates background information on Rowan Atkinson / Mr Bean.
2	Prep work	• The communicative situation of the clip is introduced: who, where, what. • A few key phrases may be pre-taught.
3	1st purpose	T announces that the presentation of the film will be stopped three times in order to elicit feedback from the S.
4	1st viewing	The whole film is shown, the pause button is pressed at the following points, and S have to guess: • 0:29 (»Tommy is in trouble«): what trouble? • 0:52 (»If he wasn't dead, I'd have him expelled«): why dead? • 3:46 (»I've been pulling your leg«): what punchline?
5	Global comprehension	With each freeze frame, answers from the S are collected.
6	2nd purpose	S are asked to focus on the different sources of humour during the second viewing of this skit.
7	2nd viewing	The video is presented straight through.
8	Detailed comprehension	S answers on humour are discussed.
9	3rd viewing	A subtitled version of the video with several spelling and lexical mistakes is shown, and S are asked to shout »Stop!« whenever they identify a mistake. The correct versions are written on the board.
10	Wrap-up	The appropriateness of this video concerning its content and the role of black humour are discussed.

Fig. 11: *Fatal Beatings*

While this 10-step model is intended to foster the first two skills of short film literacy (see Fig. 8), promoting the third skill, i.e. creating, can be guided by the 10-level pyramid, in which the autonomous production of a short film by the learners takes centre stage (Fig. 12).

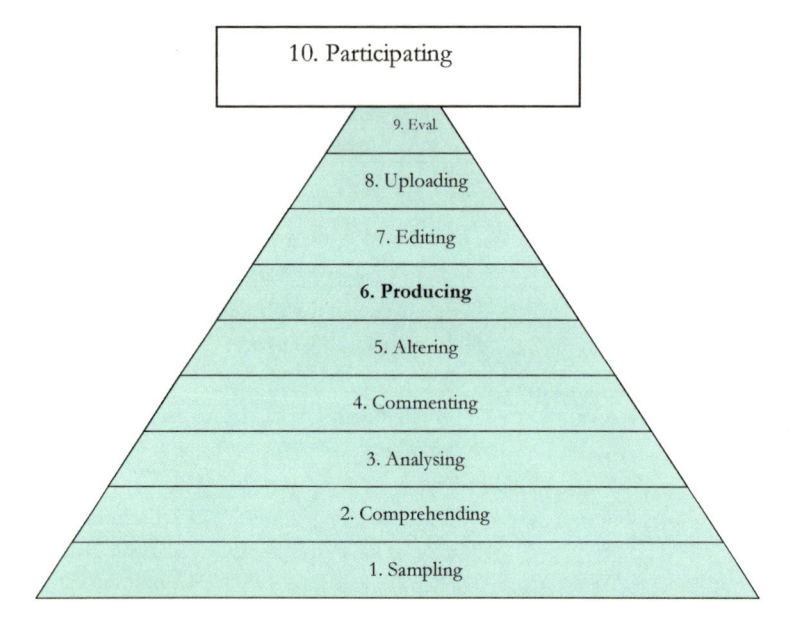

```
10. Participating
 9. Eval.
 8. Uploading
 7. Editing
 6. Producing
 5. Altering
 4. Commenting
 3. Analysing
 2. Comprehending
 1. Sampling
```

Fig. 12: Ten – Level Pyramid

8 Conclusion

When employing short films in TEFL, teachers should resort to *Balanced Teaching*, i.e. a synthesis of closed and open methods (Thaler 2008). Fig. 13 elucidates how this basic approach can be adapted for short films.

Balanced Teaching		
Closed Teaching		Open Learning
• teacher-fronted • cinematic analysis • closed exercises • one film • deskbound approach	&	• student-centred • listening-viewing for gist • open tasks • intermediality • independent study
motivating & effective TEFL		

Fig. 13: *Balanced Teaching* with short films

Bibliography

Donaghy, Kieran (2015). Film in Action. Peaslake: Delta Publishing.
Heinrich, Katrin (1997). Der Kurzfilm. Geschichte, Gattungen, Narrativik. Alfeld: Coppi.
Keddie, Jamie (2014). Bringing Online Video into the Classroom. Oxford: Oxford University Press.
KMK (Hg.) (2003). Bildungsstandards mittlerer Schulabschluss. www.kmk.org/fileadmin/veroeffentlichungen_beschluesse/2003/2003_12_0 4-BS-erste-Fremdsprache.pdf
KMK (Hg.) (2012). Bildungsstandards allgemeine Hochschulreife. www.kmk.org/fileadmin/veroeffentlichungen_beschluesse/2012/2012_10_18-Bildungsstandards-Fortgef-FS-Abi.pdf
Monaco, James (2009). How to Read a Film. Oxford: Oxford University Press.
Stempleski, Susan / Tomalin, Barry (2001). Film. Oxford: Oxford University Press.
Thaler, Engelbert (2016). Kurzfilme im Fremdsprachenunterricht. Praxis Fremdsprachenunterricht 6, 7–11.
Thaler, Engelbert (2015). Literal Music Videos. Praxis Fremdsprachenunterricht 3, 6–7.
Thaler, Engelbert (2014). Teaching English with Films. Paderborn: UTB.
Thaler, Engelbert (2012). Englisch unterrichten. Berlin: Cornelsen.
Thaler, Engelbert (2008). Offene Lernarrangements im Englischunterricht. Berlin: Langenscheidt.
Thaler, Engelbert (2007a). Film-based Language Learning. Praxis Fremdsprachenunterricht 1, 9–14.
Thaler, Engelbert (2007b). Schulung des Hör-Seh-Verstehens. Praxis Fremdsprachenunterricht 4, 12–17.
Thaler, Engelbert (2000). Monty Python. Paderborn: Schöningh.

Goose Bumps – How the Language of Film Enters into Language Teaching with Films

Klaus Maiwald

Part 1 of the following article outlines didactic reasons and directions of working with films and short films. Part 2 will take a closer look at the innertextual and intertextual qualities of a particular short film, showing how the language of film, its formal means and aesthetic techniques, is integral to language learning with film. Part 3 concludes that while film analysis is no end in itself, it is required in defining and fulfilling language oriented tasks.

1 Didactic Reasons and Directions of Working with (Short) Films

Why work with (short) films in language teaching? A simple answer to that question is: because they exist. We study music; we study painting; we study architecture; we study literature; so we study film. (We might even consider film a form of literature.) In any case, film is an art form with a history spanning well over a hundred years (see Faulstich 2005). Film has developed genuine aesthetic codes, for example cut and montage, and specific genres, for example the Western, the Road Movie, the Thriller (see Hickethier 2007: 201 ff.; Kammerer 2009). And film has brought forth renowned auteurs and œuvres – or slightly less pretentious: film makers and works. Think about Sergei Eisenstein, Alfred Hitchcock, Stanley Kubrick, Woody Allen, to name but a few. In his voluminous yet highly readable study *The Big Screen. The Story of the Movies and What They Did to Us*, David Thomson (2012) traces more than a century in which films have been shaping our thoughts and feelings, about the world and ourselves. If one purpose of higher education is to open up legitimate cultural objects and processes, there is no way around film – unless we exclude film from an elitist concept of a supposed »high culture«.

To pronounce film a legitimate part of our culture and the cultural heritage (*Bildungsgut*) is all very well. Yet in these days, education aims not so much at cultural goods (like Shakespeare's sonnets or Beethoven's symphonies) but at abilities and skills which enable us to fulfill tasks, to solve problems, to cope with our lives. This focus on competences rather than contents is basically a sound idea. Cluttering up one's mind with declarative knowledge makes little sense in a world in which knowledge evolves rapidly and becomes obsolete fast.

On the other hand, competence-oriented education poses a latent threat to all things lacking immediate usefulness and to all abilities that have no tangible and measurable outcome. Art is such a thing; aesthetic sensitivity is such an ability. So why deal with films?

If the idea of film as a learning object will not suffice, film certainly qualifies as a learning medium, especially in teaching foreign languages and cultures:

- Characters in foreign films speak foreign languages, so film may be used for listening to authentic native speakers.
- Although films are never reflections but always models of reality (see Surkamp 2010: 94), they still convey images of historical or contemporary realities. We watch the melodrama FAR FROM HEAVEN (2002) and get an idea of what 1950s' suburban culture in the U.S. was like. We watch HOUSE OF CARDS (2013 to present) and get an idea of how contemporary politics and government (probably, and horribly) work in the U.S.[1]
- Films call for explanation and interpretation and thus provide occasions for speaking, reading, and writing: Is the ending in FAR FROM HEAVEN a happy one? What keeps the couple Frank and Claire in HOUSE OF CARDS together?

But neither FAR FROM HEAVEN nor HOUSE OF CARDS are short films. Short films can be defined as films not exceeding 30 minutes in duration (see Behrendt 2011: 396). Film history began with very short short films. Due to technical limitations early films (most notably by the brothers Lumière) would not even exceed one minute; and they were mainly used as entertainment attractions at vaudevilles and fun fares. Today, shortness is not so much a technical necessity but an artistic choice. And short films are no longer a means of ›lowly‹ mass amusement but rather a domain of ›high-brow‹ expertise. Apart from commercials, music videos, and the like, short films are no part of the popular cultural mainstream. They tend to appear at specialized festivals (e.g. *Oberhausener Kurzfilmtage*), on quality television, and usually far removed from prime time slots (see Abraham 2013: 7).

If short films occupy cultural margins, why give them center (or any) stage in education?[2] For one thing, public education is not merely to replicate cultural practices and aesthetic experiences students know from their everyday lives. Public education is to broaden and to deepen those practices and experiences. School is the place where especially children and young adults from underprivileged educational backgrounds (*bildungsfern*) may access cultural spheres

---

1 See filmography at the end of the article.
2 The same question would apply to poetry and short fiction, which in our classrooms enjoy a presence completely out of proportion with their presence in literary culture.

otherwise beyond their reach: the library, the theater, the short film. A more pragmatic, if not trivial, reason for dealing with short films lies in their brevity. A full-length movie such as FAR FROM HEAVEN and even more so more than 50 episodes of HOUSE OF CARDS are hard to fit into the time frames of everyday teaching. The necessity turns into virtue, though, as precisely for their shortness, short films may be especially rich learning objects. Let us look at a case in point.

2 A Short Film as Rich Learning Object

2.1 Innertextual Aspects

Here is the story: It is a dark, rainy and thundery night. A man is sitting in the shelter of a tram stop. Out of nowhere appears an attractive woman, in an elegant dress. The man is about to help her out with some small change for the ticket machine and, seeing her freezing and with goose bumps, takes off his jacket – but leaves it at that. The man's next moves to make contact also fail. The woman manages to light her cigarette without his assistance, and before he needs hers, he finds his own matches. His attempt to offer and hand her his jacket is cut short by a blackout in the shelter. When the lights turn on again, the opportunity is gone somehow and the man is clinging to his jacket again. The camera pulls back from the characters, indicating distance; a sequence of somewhat melancholy guitar chords underscores the failed attempt at communication and contact. As if to signify the end of all hopes, the man grinds out his cigarette butt. He then notices some laughter whose source is not visible on-screen but is obviously nearby on-scene. The camera moves to a long close-up of the man's face, which finally breaks into a smile. He turns and extends his jacket towards the woman. But she has just left the scene and steps into the departing tram. The doors shut; the tram starts moving.

The film thus far very much works like a short story. There is no exposition; we get a slice of the everyday life of (seemingly) ordinary people; there is an open ending. We start out with the greatest of all possible plot triggers: boy meets girl. But then, nothing really happens (Fig. 1):

Fig. 1: Boy meets girl – with nothing happening (0:03:26)

There is no third person, no erotic competition in a so-called love triangle. These two do not unleash animal instincts for sex on the spot. There is no high-pitched scream out of the blackout as she is being slashed and slaughtered by the infamous tram-stop-killer. The woman, for her part, does not turn out to be some psychosexual maniac like Glenn Close in Adrian Lyne's FATAL ATTRACTION (1987). These two do not even talk, for heaven's sake! A man and a woman, roughly the same age, both decent- to good-looking, both smokers, both stranded at some forsaken tram stop. Why can't he just hand her his jacket, saying something like: »You must be freezing – want my jacket for a while?« The man acts inhibited, perhaps intimidated by her flashiness and self-assurance. His gingerly efforts to establish contact – the small change, the matches, the jacket – they all fail. Even smoking provides no ground for some harmless talk.

A useful task here would be to describe and to characterize the protagonists, perhaps like this: While the man is a »regular guy«, average, shy, timid, the woman comes across flashy, extravagant (note her dress, and she also sports a tattoo on her arm), self-assured, perhaps even a bit perky. Explaining the characters and their quiet drama also has to take into account some means of filmic representation: First of all, the fictional world is in black and white, not colorful and vivid. Secondly, music and camera movement structure the sequence of events. Each time an effort at making contact has failed, the camera pulls back (from the take we see in Fig. 1) into a medium long shot, while a sequence of elegiac guitar chords can be heard. Thirdly, close-ups and detail shots are used for emphasis: the woman's goose bumps and their close perception by the man through subjective camera; or the grinding out of a cigarette butt.

Camera movement, field size and shot length combine suggestively when the man notices the nearby laughter. The film takes ten long seconds to zoom into a close-up of the man's face and it holds that close-up for another eight seconds before the man starts smiling. It is often held against film that everything is shown and therefore nothing left to imagine, no gaps to be filled in. Here is a striking example to the contrary: What is going on in the man's mind at this moment? Let us fill an imaginary thought bubble: *»Man, those guys seem to be having some fun. And I can't even speak to this nice woman, who is obviously freezing? What is my problem? Why can't I give her my goddamn jacket? Jesus, what is wrong with me? Now come on!«*

We see how the language of film enters into language teaching with films. Our average high school student will not aspire to be a film critic or a film scholar. So it makes but little sense to systematically analyze the visual, the auditive, and the narrative qualities of a given film take by take, scene by scene.³ On the other hand, understanding content cannot discount form, that is, the way a story is constructed in the audiovisual medium, that is, the language of film.

The ending described so far is an open one. How will the story go on? Will our man succumb to quiet desperation, wait for the next tram, ride home and continue a lonely life? Not unlikely. Will he commit some act of violence, against himself or against the nearby laughers? Hardly. Will he haste after the woman, join her in the tram? Perhaps. Will they keep speechless and distant, or will they talk? Hard to tell. What will they talk about? Even harder to tell. Will they part as casual acquaintances? To be expected. Or will they have found the love of their lives, get married and live happily ever after? Probably not. The ending is open, but the subdued, laconic »language« of this film makes some endings more likely than others.

Here is the ending: After turning around from the laughter and realizing that the woman has gone, the man also takes off – whether to make the tram or run after the woman remains unclear. In any case, he ends up not in the same coach with the woman, but in another one. Leaning forward and resting his head on his elbows, he disappears from view as the train sets in motion from right to left (Fig. 2).

Fig. 2: Final view of the protagonist (0:07:05)

More than a hearty determination this motion indicates a quiet resignation. Ironically, the jacket the man would or could not part with has been left behind in the shelter. The ending still remains open, but it seems unlikely that anything will develop between him and her. Once again the *leitmotif* of the guitar chords

---

3   To distinguish between the visual, the auditive, and the narrative is quite common in film analysis. See for example Hickethier (2007: 37–160) or Frederking / Krommer / Maiwald (2012: 177–186).
    Useful online resources for film analysis in English are, for example, the Australian Centre for the Moving Image (Ed.), Liebelt (2003), and Universität Wien (Ed.).

can be heard. Also, the tram moves from right to left, which in our culture is a backward, not a forward move. On the other hand, the man has overcome his passivity and parted with his jacket. Maybe he has learned something and will change somewhat. Also, there is something new in the music, that is, a simple tune whistled above the chords. This well-crafted, detail-rich, and ambiguous ending demands close attention to filmic means, and it invites further interpretation: What, if anything, will come of it?

So far, I have left out the beginning of this film because the opening sequence requires ›higher‹ analysis and interpretation beyond the merely inner-textual content.

2.2 Intertextuality

The protagonist comes out of a movie theater which advertises A STREETCAR NAMED DESIRE as that night's feature film. He is being discharged into a dark night and rolling thunder. One last cigarette lit, then the doors close, and the lights go out (Fig. 3). The man strolls past a movie poster of BEN HUR, waves off a taxi and then walks across the street towards the tram stop.

Fig. 3: From the movies into reality (0:00:58)

The intertextual references are too suggestive to be accidental. A STREETCAR NAMED DESIRE is Elia Kazan's 1951 film based on the play by Tennessee Williams (1947). It is about an aging and fragile woman who in a futile and fatal manner clings to a long lost world of memories and illusions.[4] While A STREETCAR NAMED DESIRE is about an unfulfilled and failed life, BEN HUR is the exact opposite.

---

4   Blanche DuBois (played by Vivian Leigh) seeks refuge at her younger sister's in New Orleans. She still acts the refined and delicate Southern belle when in fact her life is a shambles: The family plantation is lost; her marriage has failed; she had to quit her teaching job because of an affair with a student; she has a serious alcohol problem; she is broke and has nowhere to go. In the course of events she gets raped by her brutal brother-in-law Stanley Kowalski, and a last potential suitor turns away when he learns about her past.

William Wyler's 1959 film, a prime example of the sword-and-sandal genre, recounts the life of a man of action (aptly played by Charlton Heston), who endures and prevails by force of will and brain and muscle.

How do these films tie in with our film? For once, our protagonist is the utmost ironic opposite of Ben Hur. He has retreated from reality into the cinema to take in a melancholic melodrama. After the gates to the dream world have closed, he indulges in a cigarette and some afterthought before reality is calling from across the street in the form of a starkly lit tram station, where streetcars are not poetically named *Desire* but prosaically »No. 3«. The references to A STREETCAR NAMED DESIRE and BEN HUR thus suggest an interpretation of the main character: Here is a person to whom the cinema and the movies are surrogates for things missing in his life.

That is why the woman coming out of nowhere in the dark is so unsettling. Elegant, debonair, attractive, and self-confident, she looks as if descended straight from a movie screen. Except she is no apparition; she is the real thing. The way she is presented – in black and white, wearing an off-the-shoulder dress, smoking casually, sporting a tattoo – implies yet another intertextual reference, to the Hollywood genre of the *film noir* (Fig. 4). The classic period of the film noir lasted from the early 1940s to the late 1950s. *Film noir* stories typically center on sex and crime, stock figures of the genre being the hardboiled, cynical detective and a mysterious and lascivious femme fatale. The signal film of the genre was DOUBLE INDEMNITY (1944) by Billy Wilder, starring Barbara Stanwyck.

Fig. 4: Genre reference to *film noir* (0:04:19) (right: Barbara Stanwyck in DOUBLE INDEMNITY[5])

Clearly, our smoking beauty is a genre reference to the *film noir*, which once again calls up and deepens the ironic contrast between the histrionic glamour on the movie screen and the trite realities of waiting for a tram. The film references (in combination with the *mise en scène*) conjure up expectations of tragic

---

5   https://sites.tufts.edu/filmnoirntaxis01/2015/05/02/double-indemnity-an-exploration-of-exigencies-for-agency (26.10.2016)

romance, rough adventure, and erotic promise in a reality where nothing of all that materializes.

2.3 Summary

The innertextual make-up and the intertextual references account for a complex film, a rich aesthetic learning object. But alas! The characters in this short film remain speechless. No authentic native speaker material here. Also, this film is not set in an English-speaking environment, so there is nothing to learn about country and people, habits and customs. Our film is Swiss, its director is Laszlo Kish, its original title is GÄNSEHAUT (goose bumps). The story is rather archetypal, though, and clearly this 8-minute-film succeeds in packing a lot of meaning into a very small space. It employs well-wrought narrative patterns such as the division into three distinct parts (exposition in front of the cinema, main part in the shelter, coda in the tram), a careful structuring of space (with a street separating the illusionist world of the cinema from the real world of public transportation), and the best of all possible complications: the appearance of a woman[6]. More importantly, this film makes very effective use of the genuine language of film, which is not verbal but audiovisual: the black and white, the music (off scene) and the laughter (off screen), camera movement, field size, shot length. Last but not least, the meaning of this film draws heavily on intertextual references and ironies: A STREETCAR NAMED DESIRE, BEN HUR, the *film noir*. Like in a good poem or short story there is a density of aesthetic means and the kind of over-structuring we know to be the hallmarks of poetic texts.

3 Conclusion: Film Analysis and (Language) Tasks

But once again: Film analysis is no end in itself, especially in language teaching. Above all, language teaching is about language skills, that is: speaking, writing, reading, listening. Our film offers many occasions for exercising those skills, ranging broadly from analytical to imaginative (Fig. 5):

Treating films in language teaching will focus on tasks like these rather than on systematic film analysis. On the other hand, tasks like these cannot be defined let alone fulfilled without attention to the means and techniques of the medium, without decoding its language. This does not mean that language teachers need to be film scholars to boot. It does mean, however, that a basic ability to »read« films should be a part of language teacher education.

---

[6] Apart from Glenn Close in FATAL ATTRACTION, see for example Marilyn Monroe in THE SEVEN YEAR ITCH (1955) or, on the darker side, Elizabeth Taylor in A PLACE IN THE SUN (1951) and Jessica Lange in THE POSTMAN ALWAYS RINGS TWICE (1981).

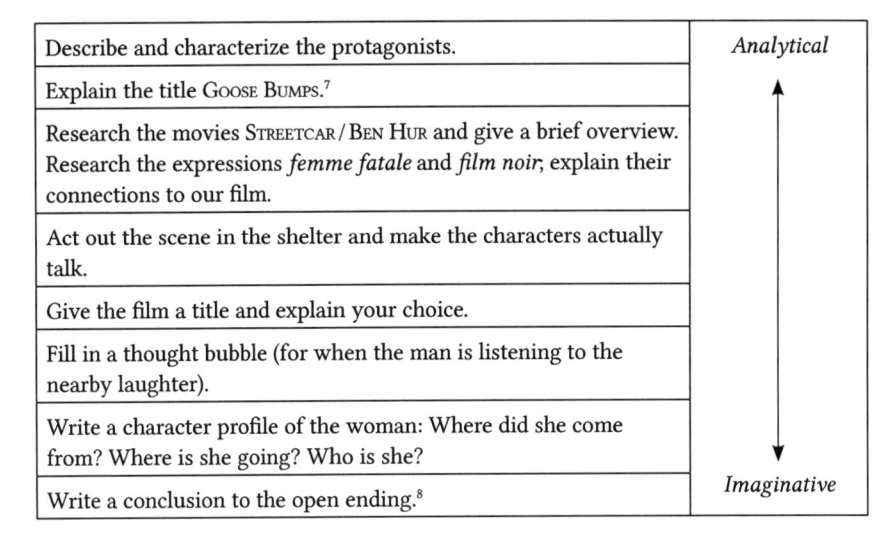

Describe and characterize the protagonists.	*Analytical*
Explain the title GOOSE BUMPS.[7]	▲
Research the movies STREETCAR / BEN HUR and give a brief overview. Research the expressions *femme fatale* and *film noir*, explain their connections to our film.	
Act out the scene in the shelter and make the characters actually talk.	
Give the film a title and explain your choice.	
Fill in a thought bubble (for when the man is listening to the nearby laughter).	
Write a character profile of the woman: Where did she come from? Where is she going? Who is she?	▼
Write a conclusion to the open ending.[8]	*Imaginative*

Fig. 5: Tasks ranging from analytical to imaginative

Bibliography

Print / Internet Sources

Abraham, Ulf (2013). Kurzspielfilme im Deutschunterricht. In: Praxis Deutsch 237. Seelze: Friedrich Verlag, 4–14.
Australian Centre for the Moving Image (Ed.). Guide to Film Analysis in the Classroom. Available at http://www.adelaidefestivalcentre.com.au/media/3750/film-analysis-in-classroom.pdf (Stand: 26.10.2016)
Behrendt, Esther Maxine (2011). Kurzfilm. In: Koebner, Thomas (Ed.). Sachlexikon des Films. 3rd ed. Stuttgart: Reclam, 396–398.
Faulstich, Werner (2005). Filmgeschichte. Paderborn: Wilhelm Fink.
Frederking, Volker / Krommer, Axel / Maiwald, Klaus (2012). Mediendidaktik Deutsch. Eine Einführung. 2nd, revised ed. Berlin: Erich Schmidt.
Hickethier, Knut (2007). Film- und Fernsehanalyse. 4th ed. Stuttgart: Metzler.
Kammerer, Ingo (2009). Film – Genre – Werkstatt. Baltmannsweiler: Schneider.
Klant, Michael (2012). Grundkurs Film 3: Die besten Kurzfilme: Materialien für die Sek I und II. Braunschweig: Schroedel.

---

[7] Does the title merely refer to the woman's literal goose bumps? Or to the man's invisible / metaphorical ones? Or do we get goose bumps from watching this film?
[8] The endings should of course not flow from unbound »creativity« but be consistent with the characters and the story.

Liebelt, Wolf (2003). The Language of Film. Fachausdrücke, Interpretationsfragen und Redemittellisten für die Arbeit mit Filmen im Englischunterricht. Available at http://www.nibis.de/nli1/bibl/pdf/tfm06.pdf (Stand: 26.10.2016)

Surkamp, Carola (2010). Zur Bedeutung der Schulung filmästhetischer Kompetenz aus der Sicht unterschiedlicher Fächer. In: Kepser, Matthis (Ed.). Fächer der schulischen Filmbildung. München: Kopaed, 85–108.

Thomson, David (2012). The Big Screen. The Story of the Movies and What They Did to Us. New York: Farrar, Straus and Giroux.

Universität Wien (Ed.). Begriffslexikon FILM der Universität Wien. Available at https://wiki.univie.ac.at/display/filex/Startseite (Stand: 26.10.2016)

Film

A PLACE IN THE SUN (George Stevens, USA 1951)
A STREETCAR NAMEND DESIRE (Elia Kazan, USA 1951)
BEN HUR (William Wyler, USA 1959)
DOUBLE INDEMNITY (Billy Wilder, USA 1944)
FAR FROM HEAVEN (Todd Haynes, USA 2002)
FATAL ATTRACTION (Adrian Lyne, USA 1987)
GÄNSEHAUT (Laszlo I. Kish, CH 1993) (available at http://www.youtube.com/watch?v=5NLpiyDmfVM) (Stand: 26.10.2016)
HOUSE OF CARDS (USA 2013 ff.)
THE POSTMAN ALWAYS RINGS TWICE (Bob Rafelson, USA 1981)
THE SEVEN YEAR ITCH (Billy Wilder, USA 1955)

Afrofuturist Interventions into the Postcolonial: Wanuri Kahiu's *Pumzi*

Annika McPherson

Water scarcity, access to clean water and other concerns surrounding the sustainability of global and regional water supplies have long featured prominently in environmental political activism as well as in ecocritical and ecofeminist creative interventions. Especially in relation to those regions of the Global South where these issues are of great urgency, such interventions frequently point to the legacies of colonial and ongoing labor exploitation and resource extraction.

In a similar vein, since early 2016 indigenous water protectors at Standing Rock have been resisting the construction of the Dakota Access Pipeline, which is supposed to transport oil over the boundaries of tribal lands, violating sacred sites and substantially increasing the risk of environmental disasters in its wake. Invoking the principle ›Mni Wiconi‹ (›Water is Life‹),[1] the water protectors drew worldwide attention and mobilized solidarity and support not least through social media technology. Globally, other community and environmental activist confrontations with capital and militarized police forces face similar challenges, while resource conflicts resulting from climate change are also on the rise, not least because more and more people become displaced as environmental migrants or climate refugees.

Taking its cue from the theme of water scarcity and resource conflicts, Kenyan writer and director Wanuri Kahiu's award-winning 2009 short film *Pumzi* (›Breath‹ in Swahili) is set in the dystopian »Maitu Community, East African Territory, 35 years after World War III – The Water War,«[2] as indicated by the introductory textual overlay. The film's establishing shot zooms in on the community's self-sustaining and hermetically sealed off architectural structure, the design of which invokes a space station, in the middle of an uninhabitable desert. We witness how Asha, the curator of the Virtual Natural History Museum, dreams of a lush green tree in the midst of the desert and, following protocol and instructions by the dream detecting technology, uses »dream suppressants« to prevent further dreaming. In her dream, Asha has facial decorations and wears different clothes, which suggests a desire for or memory of alternative ways of

---

1 http://standwithstandingrock.net/mni-wiconi/.
2 In Kikuyu ›Maitū‹ means ›mother‹ in reference to one's own mother.

being than those within the Maitu community structure. The order to suppress dreams indicates that dreaming, especially of alternative ways of life, poses a threat to the established authoritarian structure of the community of survivors. Shortly after this scene, Asha receives a package with an unmarked soil sample and discovers its viability. She begins to question the claim that »the outside is dead,« as the Maitu Council responds to her request for an exit visa. Echoed in the tag line, »the outside is dead« frames the film's theme of hope and sacrifice in the wake of ecological disaster and post-war authoritarian social reconfiguration, and Asha's search for ecological viability resonates with broader questions of agency and power.

To date, *Pumzi* has mainly been discussed either in relation to its environmental theme and ecofeminist critique (Calvin 2014) or within the broader context of »Postcrisis African Science Fiction« (Omelsky 2014). Andrea Hurston, in turn, emphasizes the film's futurism through the invocation of ancestral ghosts as »sacred/demonic tricksters who provide alternate perspectives« onto both the present and the future (2016: 7). Bringing together and building upon these readings, the following discussion highlights the film's Afrofuturist dimension. It draws on cultural studies and postcolonial studies frameworks in order to show how broader questions of agency surrounding cultural power and cultural politics can be addressed through the analysis and discussion of *Pumzi* in educational contexts.

1 Cultural Analyses of Power, Politics, and Culture

Adopting the perspective of cultural studies, this essay analyzes the award-winning 2009 short film *Pumzi*. Building upon different readings of the film, it highlights its Afrofuturist dimension by drawing on cultural studies and postcolonial studies frameworks.

In the words of Henry A. Giroux, cultural studies' inquiries into »the interrelationship of power, politics, and culture« continue to be highly relevant in educational contexts because of their »promise [of] a larger transformative and democratic politics« (2004: 59). Critical analyses of the symbolic and institutional entanglements of culture and power understand culture as »partly defined as a circuit of power, ideologies, and values in which diverse images and sounds are produced and circulated, identities are constructed, inhabited, and discarded, agency is manifested in both individualized and social forms, and discourses are created« (Giroux 2004: 59–60). Hence, culture can be seen as »an educational site where identities are being continually transformed, power is enacted, and learning assumes a political dynamic as it becomes not only the condition for the acquisition of agency but also the sphere for imagining oppositional social change« (Giroux 2004: 60).

Entanglements of the symbolic and the institutional in this context are frequently analyzed through popular culture material, although, as John Storey phrases it, »popular culture is in effect an *empty* conceptual category« that can be variously used in different contexts (2008: 1). Since the late 1950s, cultural studies has been instrumental in challenging the ›high culture‹/›popular culture‹ divide by tracing how notions of culture have informed, for example, the discursive construction of the nation and concurrent processes of social inclusion and exclusion or political containment. The signifying practices of culture can be explored in the realm of the ›popular‹ in the sense of what Raymond Williams has famously called a »particular way of life, whether of a people, a period or a group« (cited in Storey 2001: 2). This can be applied not only to the lived culture of, for example, specific youth cultures, but also to those »ways of life« represented and imaginatively constructed in literary, filmic, and other cultural texts and practices. Hence, although it is notoriously difficult to delimit, popular culture in cultural studies is considered »a profoundly political concept« (Storey 2001: 12), which – according to some critics – is what distinguishes it from more abstract postmodern interventions into the ›high culture‹/›popular culture‹ division.

According to Williams, any culture furthermore features »dominant,« »residual« and »emergent« practices (2009: 121–127). For example, »certain experiences, meanings, and values« that are lived or circulate in the present and were formed in the past are »still active in the cultural process« of signification as »residual« elements, which can have »an alternative or even oppositional relation to the dominant culture,« but can also have been »wholly or largely incorporated« into it (Williams 2009: 122). »Emergent,« in turn, relates to the creation of »new meanings and values, new practices, new relationships and kinds of relationship« that are »substantially alternative or oppositional« to the »dominant« culture (Williams 2009: 123).

As far as the reception of televisual material is concerned, cultural theorist Stuart Hall, in his frequently cited essay »Encoding/Decoding,« suggests three positions from which such decodings can be constructed: the *dominant-hegemonic*, the *negotiated* and the *oppositional position* (1999: 515–17). According to this theoretical model of reception, viewers can decode messages in terms of the reference code of their encoding and thus operate in agreement with »what has been dominantly defined and professionally signified« (Hall 1999: 515–16). Negotiated decoding, in turn, »contains a mixture of adaptive and oppositional elements« and may appear contradictory because it operates through »particular or situated logics,« while oppositional positioning decodes messages in a contrary way »within some alternative framework or reference« (Hall 1999: 516-17). Beyond the immediate context of news broadcasting in which this model was originally developed and applied, different positions of reception can also be used to think about and discuss questions of categorization and labelling in audiovisual cultural representation.

Cultural analyses elaborate such practices and possible positions of reading and viewing of different types and genres of cultural texts and popular culture material. In doing so, they assume »an interaction between the discourses of the text and the discourses of the reader,« as Storey has phrased it in reference to David Morley's (1992) elaboration of Hall's model (Storey 2001:11). Bearing in mind the categorical indeterminacy of ›popular culture‹ and that readings and analyses are always marked by subjectivity in relation to a variety of social factors and critical frameworks, what happens when we shift the label and analytical lens from ›science fiction‹ to the currently very trendy term ›Afrofuturism‹? Genre labels and categories are positioned differently towards discursive conventions and can draw from different knowledge frameworks. In the case of *Pumzi*, how can ›ecofeminist science fiction‹ be related to broader questions of agency, cultural power and cultural politics within an Afrofuturist framework?

2 From Science Fiction to Afrofuturism and Back

Afrofuturist ideas and aesthetics can be observed across a wide range of cultural expressions and political practices as well as across different media and genres ranging from literary texts to blogs, film, music, and visual arts. They highlight subject positions and subjectivities that resist dominant Eurocentric conceptualizations of the future. Afrofuturism thus uses 20th and 21st century technocultures as tools for envisaging alternative futures in relation to both the political present and the past (see also Dery 1994: 180). It often engages Afrocentric perspectives and imaginaries in response to and as a form of resistance against histories, politics, and aesthetics that centre European knowledge frameworks. Hence, it is intricately entwined with questions of social as well as cultural power and politics, which can be illustrated by incorporating interview and presentation material into the discussion of *Pumzi*'s genre in educational settings.

Ritch Calvin's discussion of *Pumzi* places the film within the science fiction mode (2014: 22-23), which concurs with Kahiu's statement in an interview by Oulimata Gueye (2013). Kahiu explains that the film's science fiction aesthetics resulted from a decision based on the producer's input due to the story's futuristic setting. To Kahiu, the story, which initially had featured more fantasy elements, outweighed the interpretive frame or genre. But the film's eventual aesthetics certainly resonated with a popular trend, and it circulated widely on- and offline after having toured many film festivals. When asked about the perceived recent trend of science fiction from the African continent, Kahiu points out increased technological possibilities and wider continental exposure to different genres, but challenges the assumption of newness:

> »I don't think we've just started. I think that science fiction has been a genre in Africa that has been used a lot for a long period of time [...]. And if we think about science fiction as the use of science or something that is fictitiously science or speculative fiction within a story, then we've always used it, because we've used botany, we've used entomology, the idea of the study of animals to tell stories, or the ideas of insects to tell stories, or the idea of natural sciences and using trees – that's all science fiction [...]. I think the difference now is that people have more access to Africa and are better able to hear more stories coming out of Africa. I don't think the stories are new. I don't think that science fiction is a new genre, just I like I don't think fantasy is a new genre in Africa. It has always existed. It's how we have told stories to our children, it's how we have communicated morality and tradition and a code of conduct and how to behave and how to be part of the society. The use of futurism and the use of speculative fiction [...] may seem like it's becoming a trend, but [...] I think in every culture that I've heard of, there have always been people in all parts of Africa that have either looked to space or have had people who are seers, who could see into the future and who could disseminate the future and tell people what is going to happen – so we've always been able to draw from things that are outside of this world to be able to make sense of what's inside of the world« (Kahiu 2013, 1:48–4:03).[3]

In this comment, science fiction is aligned with natural sciences, while the speculative mode in storytelling is re-framed as a long-standing element of African narrative genres imbued with questions of morality and social codes of conduct. Looking to space, outward and inward and into the future for spiritual or moral guidance thus becomes part of social and cultural processes of making sense of the world and creating meaning.

One frequently pointed out example of looking to space and drawing from things that are outside of this world is Dogon cosmology. To the perplexity of and continuous controversy among anthropologists, the ethnographically recorded cosmological knowledge of the Dogon of Mali predated the technological possibilities of observation of the Sirius star system, a fact which led to diverging interpretations of their narratives of extraterrestrial visitors. Discrepant truth claims in explanations of this knowledge point to limited competencies in decoding complex cultural practices, narratives, and aesthetics. Accordingly, the distribution and re-mythologizing of such examples, e.g. in esoteric online circles, is accompanied by the perpetual exoticization and Othering of African

---

3   Transcriptions AM.

customs and belief systems. Kahiu also refers to the Dogon as an example of how Afrofuturism »has been part of the history of West Africa« and other African cultures in her TEDx Talk »Afrofuturism in Popular Culture« (2012, 4:40–6:04).[4]

Many artists aligned with Afrofuturism as an aesthetic practice use similar referential strategies to traditional African knowledges and modes of narration and, in doing so, expose the exclusion of this kind of knowledge from Western historiography and representations of Africa and African diasporas. Like novelist Samuel Delany, they point to the existential necessity of imagining alternative futures in response to histories of erasure and continuous socio-political and cultural marginalization:

> »Science fiction isn't just thinking about the world out there. It's also thinking about how that world might be—a particularly important exercise for those who are oppressed, because if they're going to change the world we live in, they—and all of us—have to be able to think about a world that works differently« (Delany 2011).

In the face of the representational legacies that are attributed to colonial practices of Othering and the denigration of African knowledges, Wanuri Kahiu thus calls for writers and filmmakers to be »conscious creators« and to counter the still predominantly negative imagery of ›Africa‹:

> »I think we should be conscious creators – especially [...] people of African descent, or people from an African Diaspora, or people who are on the continent, or who live outside the continent, we should be very clear about the images we are putting out of ourselves, because Black people, in general, have had a very slanted image for a long time. We've always been portrayed as violent, we've always been portrayed as victims. Women have been portrayed either as mothers or as prostitutes. [...] Because, especially coming from Africa, where all the images that have come out have been about starvation, or children with flies in their eyes, or war or destruction, or poverty, or hunger, or famine, there have been so many negative images coming out of Africa that if we don't actively combat those images we're doing ourselves a disservice – and not only for ourselves, but for future generations, and for that reason we have to be very careful about being part of a trend for the sake of being part of a trend or being part of a trend that is actually saying something« (Kahiu 2013, 5:25–7:17).

The stated ongoing need to actively combat negative images underlines the activist component of much, if not most, Afrofuturist work. The conceptualization and historical narrative of Afrofuturism, however, generally relies heavily on African American contexts and examples and has recently turned into a trend,

---

4   The TEDx event, themed »Stories by the Campfire,« was organized by Joshua Wanyama and took place in Nairobi on 14 July 2012. See https://www.ted.com/tedx/events/5993.

a development which Kahiu criticizes as a potential bandwagon effect that diminishes the function of the aesthetic as telling specific stories.

Kahiu's notion of Afrofuturism includes speculative fiction, myths, legends, science fiction and related narratives which convey a sense of »what Blackness looks like in the future, real or imagined,« as she phrases it by reference to performance artist, designer and educator Denenge Akpem (Kahiu 2012, 0:20–0:45). While it encompasses »Black people in general,« Kahiu's search for »a place for Afrofuturism in Africa« (2012, 0:36, 1:44) relates not only to »the idea of using spiritualism or mythical realism within storytelling,« as e.g. in Ben Okri's fiction, but also to the everyday use of technology (2012, 3:25–4:07). Beyond the aspect of exercising agency in projecting one's future in response to historiographical voicelessness, Kahiu points to examples of an »Afrofuturist sense of using technology« to »run [...] everyday things« (2012, 10:10–10:59) by reference to AfriGadget.[5]

However, as a mere label, ›Afrofuturist‹ can also be ambiguous in that it potentially perpetuates Otherization:

> »There's every reason to have pop culture, and we do have a pop culture, [...] but you have to know that in everything that you make, you're making a statement, that people will perceive of it as a Black person, unfortunately. [...] If I was European I wouldn't be specifically targeted, they wouldn't specifically target the place that I am to be able to define what kind of work I'm doing. But that's different for us, especially as people of African descent. People will target it and they'll label it and will put it in a little box and say, well, that's Black art or that's African art, or that's very specific. My work is being called Afrofuturist, it is not being called science fiction. It's being called Afrofuturist to put it in a box where it's understandable to people that it comes from a Black person or it comes from an African person or a person of African descent« (Kahiu 2013, 7:23–8:36).

When used as yet another qualifier and label, Afrofuturism thus can contain the aesthetic product within hegemonic structures in that it becomes categorically excluded from the possibility of being received as mainstream science fiction. In educational settings, this ambiguity can be discussed both in terms of genre and in terms of agency and cultural power as well as regarding different reading positions in the context of cultural representation, production, and reception.

---

5   See https://www.facebook.com/afrigadget/.

3 *Pumzi*: Afrofuturism beyond Postcolonial Futurity

Extrapolation, a common device in utopian and science fiction writing, »examines the relationship between the (author's) present [...] and the future as an extension or exaggeration of social, political, and economic tendencies perceived in the present« (Thaler 2010: 72). Unlike Afrofuturist work which links the concern with the future more explicitly to the past, *Pumzi*'s narrative is mainly based on an extrapolating examination of the present. As Kahiu states in her TEDx Talk, Afrofuturism enabled her to »extrapolate on ideas, and thoughts, and feelings [...] about the way the world is running« (2012, 12:35–12:55).

In *Pumzi*, the theme of water scarcity has been extrapolated into an authoritarian post-war future that both resonates with and departs from the legacies of colonial power structures. The world outside of the community's built environment is said to be dead, and Asha's search for evidence to the contrary ultimately demands her self-sacrifice. The label on the jar in which the »MAITU (Mother) Seed« is displayed in the museum details the language etymology as Kikuyu, »from MAA (Truth) and ITU (Ours). OUR TRUTH« (0:45). The etymological explanation indicates that in-depth cultural knowledge seems to have been lost in everyday interaction, just as familial social structures seem to no longer exist. Since ›Maitu‹ is also the name of the community, however, the etymologically derived meanings collide. The centre of the architectural structure as seen in the beginning of the film invokes a seed and in that sense the self-sustaining community is ›mothering‹ the survivors. The community's council consists of three women, which suggests a post-war gynecratic social organization beyond masculinist formations. Given the clearly authoritarian structure, however, ›truth‹ is determined solely by those in charge and the council »silences all dissenters« through technologically mediated communication (Calvin 2014: 25). In this light, ›Maitu‹ can be read as an ironic misnomer, or at least as a doubtful claim to ›mothering‹ the community. Hence, Asha's search for the origin of the viable soil sample also constitutes a search for truth beyond the claims of the council. On her escape from silencing and surveillance Asha seems to be »channeling an ancestral memory« (Calvin 2014: 25) which guides her adaptation to the hostile outside environment.

Having found the location of the viable soil sample, with the help of which Asha had germinated the »mother seed« from the museum's specimen collection, she plants it, uses her last drops of water to nourish it, and shades it with her body to the point of self-sacrifice. However, her initial impulse to check the soil and plant the seed had stemmed from her previous foreboding dream of a lush tree in the desert and the vision of plunging into deep water that is induced when she holds the soil in her hand and smells it (5:36, see also Calvin 2014: 25).

This also suggests a reconnection with the senses that have been stifled through technological means of communication and invokes a call for re-humanization.

Asha is aided in her escape by the cleaner with whom she had previously shared some of her precious water, which indicates her sense of solidarity in the face of inequality in material distribution within the community. Watering the growing sapling during her arduous walk through the desert, Asha finally encounters the tree of her dream and vision, only to find that it is dried up and dead when she reaches it. As trees symbolize both nature and human community, the dried-up tree highlights the loss of cultural tradition and communal viability.

Yet, Asha remains hopeful and plants the sapling, her hope highlighted by the blue sky in juxtaposition to the desert. In the final and decisive time-lapse shot, she becomes the ›mother tree‹, bringing new life to the environment and, potentially, the community. Symbolically, this can invoke both the Biblical ›tree of life‹ and the ›tree of good and evil‹ (Genesis 2: 9) in that Asha's transgressive search for truth connotes righteousness and a triumph over authoritarianism. As the shot zooms out further and becomes framed by the inverted text ›PUMZI‹, however, it reveals a view onto a forest at the edge of the desert, suggesting that the truth lay just beyond Asha's grasp. Whether the forest has been there the entire time or we are seeing a further time lapse into the future remains unclear (see also Calvin 2014: 26). As tempting as it may be to frame Asha's behaviour in terms of rural African women's traditional roles as »custodians of water [...] and custodians of the earth« (Mazuri quoted in Calvin 2014: 26), the necessity of her gendered self-sacrifice leaves a troubling after-taste. *Pumzi* extrapolates colonial legacies in that it mirrors colonial practices of collection and ordering within the museum and in relation to the panoptical surveillance of dreams and actions by those in power. Asha's self-sacrifice, however, shows a decidedly tragic component which leaves ample room for different interpretations of the final shot.

Omelsky considers Asha to be an articulation of »a post-Fanonian revolutionary subject that aims to reconstitute life beyond the coercion of biopower« and the film's politics and aesthetics as expressive of »the *African* Anthropocene« in that a »continent that has been seized for nearly five hundred years by the predatory violence of imperialism, capitalism, and now global warming must see its way through to the other side of these predations—to the other side of crisis« (2014: 36).

Pumzi serves as a cautionary tale in that Asha disregards the council's prohibition to explore the outside. However, her self-sacrifice is not a punishment for her transgression, but rather is vindicated in terms of the suggested necessity to resist authoritarian power in order to ensure a sustainable future, although it rejects a »back-to-nature fantasy« (Omelsky 2014: 38). As Kahiu alerts us, Afrofuturism is not an unproblematic term in that it can perpetuate a separate ›box‹ for African cultural work, which arguably undermines the goal and desire to create a future where difference is unmarked. Furthermore, the label frequently emphasizes the work of African American artists and fails to consider the specificities of the artwork and engagements with technology on the continent.

Within the classroom or in the context of »public pedagogy,« these concerns can be aligned with broader »issues of democracy, citizenship, and the struggle over the shaping of identities and identifications« that should be taken up »as part of a larger attempt to explain how learning takes place outside of schools or what it means to assess the political significance of understanding the broader educational force of culture in the new age of media technology, multimedia, and computer-based information and communication networks« (Giroux 2004: 60).

Afrofuturism arguably tackles similar concerns regarding cultural politics and power. Yet, as every trendy topic and media form, cultural texts need to be carefully contextualized so as to avoid re-exoticization and marginalization. Addressing the problem of labelling and questioning the vocabulary of culture within different knowledge frameworks can be a first step in this direction. Accordingly, when Kahiu calls herself »a storyteller in the tradition of the Kikuyu« and describes her creative task as »a seer, not just a historian,« she alerts us to »listen to the storytellers [who] also have a voice, and their voice is important« (2012, 14:00–14:29) – both for the political present and for imaginaries of the future beyond the confines of the ›postcolonial‹.

Bibliography

Calvin, Ritch (2014). The Environmental Dominant in Wanuri Kahiu's *Pumzi*. In: Fritzsche, Sonja (ed.) The Liverpool Companion to World Science Fiction Film. Liverpool: Liverpool UP, 21–35.

Delany, Samuel R. (2011). Samuel R. Delany. The Art of Fiction No. 210. Interview by Rachel Kaadzi Ghansah. The Paris Review 197. https://www.theparisreview.org/interviews/608 8/samuel-r-delany-the-art-of-fiction-no-210-samuel-r-delany. Accessed 20 December 2016.

Dery, Mark (1994). Black to the Future: Interviews with Samuel R. Delany, Greg Tate and Tricia Rose. In: Dery, Mark (ed.) Flame Wars: The Discourse of Cyberculture. Durham and London: Duke UP, 179–222.

Giroux, Henry A. (2004). Cultural Studies, Public Pedagogy, and the Responsibility of Intellectuals. Communication and Critical/Cultural Studies 1:1, 59–79.

Hall, Stuart. Encoding/Decoding (1999). In: During, Simon (ed.) The Cultural Studies Reader. 2nd ed. London and New York: Routledge, 507–517.

Hurston, Andrea (2016). Ghost Dances on Silver Screens. Extrapolation 57:1–2, 7–20.

Kahiu, Wanuri (2012). Afrofuturism and the African. Afrofuturism in Popular Culture: Wanuri Kahiu at TEDxNairobi, 07/14/2012. TEDx Talk. https://youtu.be/PvxOL-VaV2YY?list=PLsRNoUx8w3rPra23NrMmokzCSfNsGy9KP.

Kahiu, Wanuri (2013). Africa and Science Fiction: Wanuri Kahiu's Pumzi, 2009. Interview by Oulimata Gueye at Le Moulin d'Andé. Filmed and edited by Masha Kosobokova. https://vimeo.com/104147918. Accessed 20 December 2016.

Morley, David (1992). Television, Audiences and Cultural Studies. London and New York: Routledge.

Omelsky, Matthew (2014). »After the End Times«: Postcrisis African Science Fiction. Cambridge Journal of Postcolonial Literary Inquiry 1:1, 33–49.

Pumzi (2009). Written and directed by Wanuri Kahiu. Performances by Kudzani Moswela, Chantelle Burger, Freddy Djanabia, and Anton David Jeftha. In- spired Minority Pictures.

Storey, John (2008). Cultural Theory and Popular Culture: An Introduction. 5th ed. London: Pearson/Prentice Hall.

Thaler, Ingrid (2010). Black Atlantic Speculative Fictions: Octavia E. Butler, Jewelle Gomez, and Nalo Hopkinson. New York/London: Routledge.

Williams, Raymond (repr. 2009). Marxism and Literature. Oxford and New York: Oxford University Press.

B. Methodology

Viral Videos in the EFL Classroom

Gabriele Blell

1 Introduction

Short films have flooded the Internet during the last years in the true sense of the word. Web 2.0 with its ground-breaking architecture of »participation« (O'Reilly 2005) has immensely expanded and partially radicalized our possibilities to tell and share shorts and multimedial stories of any kind with everybody. Web 2.0 has made us all consumers and producers (prosumers) at the same time (see Toffler 1980: 283). Internet platforms such as Animoto, Storybird, Windows Movie Maker, iMovie, Voicethread (Conversations in the Cloud), Monkey Jam or Audacity (see e.g. Siever 2012: 16) offer extensive tools with which everybody can tell and share short movies or other multimedia stories. Recently, various innovative formats of shorts have evolved around the idea of viralness, spreading very quickly and attaining high popularity seemingly instantaneously. Shorts have already been used in the EFL classroom for some time (see Henseler, Möller, Surkamp 2011: 147–212) because they are short, they often examine real topics and tell a story as well. Therefore, this paper treats the teaching potential of the still fairly unknown video format and phenomenon of ›viral videos‹ in school on a theoretical level (part 2 & 3), a methodological level (4), and a practical level (5). Part 2 and 3 introduce viral videos from the perspective of film studies and use the outstanding ›Yes, We Can‹ by Will.I.Am (2008) as an illustration. In part 4, methodological aspects are discussed that are useful for teaching. Finally, part 5 introduces a possible teaching scenario initiated by a complex task that has been partly designed in a university seminar and partially tested in a school classroom.

2 Viral Videos: Shorts Go Viral ...

The term ›viral video‹, first of all, is a sheer buzzword and is often used simultaneously with ›virals‹, ›viral movies‹, ›viral advertising‹, the ›viralness of videos‹, ›viral loop‹ or ›videos go viral‹. Similar to a virus in medicine, viral videos spread like an infectious disease through social networks, websites and e-mail. They become popular through the process of Web 2.0 sharing and re-sharing (see Donaghy 2015: 68). Whereas in the past, movies and videos were mostly purposefully distributed directly to the consumers only by large media organizations, DVD, TV, etc., they often gain their popularity through video-sharing today, which extends beyond the opportunity for monetization (see Broxton et. al. 2013: 242). It is the audience that decides what is good (or bad). Compared to the popularity of top stories told in print media, it becomes obvious that today any prediction on the dynamics and decentralization of viral videos follows other criteria when compared to the old ones (see Broxton et. al 2013: 242). A video's viral popularity is attained both by numerous ranking lists on the Internet (e.g. ›Viral Video Award‹) and social referrer sources (Facebook, YouTube, eBay, PayPal, Flickr, MySpace, etc.) that receive thousands and thousands of user clicks to make a short video go viral. Moreover, »(i)f videos ever went viral without marketing, it is highly unlikely that they do today« (Leopold 2009). These days, all business companies and enterprises, big and small, have monopolized the field of viral businesses and advertising and use polished marketing techniques to boost their shorts online and make their videos go viral in order to make the highest profit ever.[1] Among the techniques used are e.g. well mapped-out keywording, timing practices, astroturfing or hooking.[2] The trick is that something is created in Web 2.0 that »people *really* want so much so that their customers happily spread their product for them through their own social network of friends, family, colleagues, and peers« (Penenberg 2010: 11). What seems to be great fun on the one hand (for the majority) is big business searching for the point of nondisplacement on the Internet on the other hand (for a minority). It means that virality is incorporated into the functionality of a product (ibid.) Even the field of education has discovered viral videos with an increasing number of teaching and instruction aids on YouTube for purposeful and up-to-date and pass-it-on learning and unquestionably profit-making as well (here lies a huge field of undone research!). One result is TeacherTube, a video-sharing website for teachers, or Northwestern University offers a course on Viral Videos »YouTubing 101« with the aim of making »students savvy consumers of media artefacts« (Leopold 2009). Viralness is almost everywhere, due to the participatory feature of Web 2.0.

There is no question that viral businesses and networks have revolutionized distribution and popularization processes. They have given birth to new and innovative video formats and have been searching for new moneymaking fields in this Web of interconnectedness and interpolarity. However, since the majority of people, our students included, are active Web 2.0 participants, they have absolute

---

[1]   The well-known Tupperware parties are said to be among the oldest original viral models as well (see Penenberg 2010: 23).
[2]   'Astroturfing' means to use »multiple accounts to create what looks like grassroots ›buzz‹ about a video in the hope of bringing it to the attention of others on the Web« (Leopold 2009). ›Hooking‹ means to possibly predict (and imply) a key signifier since it is said that the video's longevity is connected with a hook that provokes the viewer to watch it (see Burgess 2008: 101-109).

access to these products and are ›invited‹ to produce and share their own videos and pass them on. Table 1 summarizes the main reasons why videos become viral. Notwithstanding the above made critical remarks, viral videos are mostly (very) short, refreshingly funny and gripping; they often examine real and provocative topics, are multimedial, last long and often put the content in a narrative nutshell, which gives them promising potential for the language class. They are provocative and search for response: confirmation or contradiction. »They're not just about puppies, college pranks and bloopers. They're also platforms for advertising, political discourse and ideas« (Leopold 2009). From the perspective of literacy orientation, learning with viral videos can support the learners' foreign-language participation in social discourses (see Hallet 2012: 10).

Shorts go viral because they ...	Notable fields of release and implications	Examples (genres)
buzz and spread very quickly, are shown repeatedly, get numerous hits	• music and band promotion • movie promotion • customer complaints (cyberbullying) • viral businesses • police misconduct • political implications (campaigning) • financial implications • advertising and marketing implycations of all kind (viral marketing) • education (TeacherTube)[3] ...	• music film • response film • branded short • how-to film • 1-second film • split-screen film • infographic film • animated lecture film • short on social issues • machinima ...
are very popular and long-lasting		
are humorous and funny (parodies, spoofs, spin-offs)		
are emotionally charged (mostly funny but also tear-jerking)		
have an uplifting content		
are mostly pervasive		
have a societal and political impact (may incriminate as well)		
have a marketability impact (advertising)		
appeal to the zeitgeist		
are multimodal (mostly combine image, language and music)		

Table 1: Features, fields and examples of viral videos (see partly O'Neill 2011 and Burgess 2008)

---

3   The Wikipedia entry https://en.wikipedia.org/wiki/Viral_video (Download 2016-09-22) gives a first summary on »Categories by subject«, which is helpful here since academic sources are rare.

It is difficult to categorize new genres for viral videos neatly. Strictly speaking, every short film can go viral, with or without marketing. At the same time, the idea of viralness may include all sorts of media and language (amount, register and various languages). However, Donaghy distinguishes nine genres in which viralness becomes manifest through (re-)sharings, revisions and juxtapositions among themselves (see Table 2). These genres meet the needs and interests of teenage learners nowadays and provide educational contexts (see Donaghy 2015: 68–72). I have added ›machinima‹ as well (Table 2; sources can be found in the bibliography).

Genre	Examples
Response film: A short commissioned by a large company that has gone viral and provoked a response video.	'Yes, We Can.' by Will.I.Am (2008). Celebrities respond to Obama's concession speech.
Branded short: A short created for a company product.	'Volkswagen. Eyes on the Road.' ›Scho-Ka-Kola‹ (2016), student project LUH; ›Come to Garbsen‹ (2016), student project LUH.
How-to film: A short which explains how things can be carried out or completed.	'How to Tie a Tie: The BEST Video to Tie a Double Windsor Knot'.
Music film: A short produced for band or music promotion.	'Psy's Gangman Style Video' (2012).
One-second film: A short that stitches important moments of life into a single chronological movie.	'One Second Everyday'. Cesar Kuijama turns favourite moments into a movie.
Split-screen film: A short (or scenes) which is divided into two halves (or three thirds / four quarters) with different moving images in each half / part.	To be seen in ›Yes, We Can‹ by Will.I.Am (2008).
Infographic film: A short graphic visual representation of information, data or knowledge.	'The Power of Food'. Infographic film about food.
Animated lecture film: A video lecture created by pairing leading experts with talented animators.	'Brené Brown on Empathy'. Lecture on empathy.

Genre	Examples
Short on social issues: A short on a social theme, such as poverty, homelessness, discrimination, etc.	'Little Chicks Take Their First Flight'. (2015) Mass killing of male chicks.
Machinima: A short made within a videogame environment.	'The Little Big Jetsons'. (The Jetsons' opening theme from 1960 recreated in Little Big Planet (Playstation 3).

Table 2: Frequently used viral video genres and examples (see partly Donaghy 2015: 68–72)

Viral videos for the language classroom can be found everywhere. Facebook users are bombarded with them every day: hit, watch and delete them, or hit, watch and post them to friends (make them go viral). Notable viral video sites are e.g. Buzzfeed (www.buzzfeed.com, available in many languages); Viral Video (viralvideoaward.com), which presents the most popular virals of a year; Google Video and, of course, YouTube, which shows users' preferences based on clicks.

3 Obama's ›Yes, We Can‹ (2008) Went Viral …

Viral businesses and strategies have also conquered other areas – like politics. Everybody may remember Barack Obama's famous concession speech in the New Hampshire Presidential Primary on 8 January 2008, in which he affirmed repeatedly that he together with all Americans would solve basic political questions like unemployment, prosperity and justice if he received their vote. In this speech he coined the influential slogan ›Yes, We Can‹.[4] His speech was frequently viewed, and it inspired musicians, artists and writers to leap and respond to this idea in their way.[5] As a result, Will.I.Am's video, ›Yes, We Can‹ (2008), went viral with more than 20 million hits and became an outstanding example of a viral video (see Penenberg 2010: 16). It is shot in black-and-white and features Obama's image in collage fashion. Approximately 40 celebrities, including musicians, singers and actors, echo his words in a hip-hop, call-and-response manner as his image and voice are played in the background using various formats of split-screening. The same happened to Will.I.Am's ›We Are the Ones‹ song (2008) (YouTube) featuring the opinions of Jessica Alba, Ryan Phil-

---

4 Although the slogan was originally coined by the United Farm Workers unionists César Chávez and Dolores Huerta in 1972 (United Farm Workers; ufw.org/_board).
5 Obama himself has always been convinced that real change comes from the bottom up. »And there's no more powerful tool for grassroots organizing than the Internet« (Penenberg 2010: 14).

lippe, Regina King and Kerry Washington. Although both videos gained widespread popularity through user-generated Internet sharing, they undoubtedly did not go viral without marketing efforts and became a tool of Obama's presidential campaign to convey his political message. Unquestionably, even Michael Moore's ›Mike's Election Guide‹ (2008) (German title: ›Yes, We Can: Mikes ultimativer Wahlführer‹) (2008) was infected and finally instrumentalized for the campaign. Interestingly, a couple of years later the video was corrupted to ›Yes, We Scan,‹ alluding to the selling of spreadshirts in the US (2013) with this slogan, which was initiated after the National Security Agency scandal about monitoring practices in the US broke. Last but not least, Chancellor Merkel was influenced by Obama's profitable slogan and modified it to ›Wir schaffen das!‹, last in her political speeches concerning the highly controversial refugee situation. Obviously, the viral success story of ›Yes, We Can‹ proves once again that the publicity outcome is predominantly a product of viral (economic and political) marketing instrumentalizing user-generated publicity. However, it also shows that the phenomenon of viralness jumps and spreads from one medium to others: video, book, (spread) shirt or language (play on words).

Yes, We Can by Will.I.Am (2008)

Fig. 1: Collage ›Yes, We Can‹ (2008–2016)

4 Viral Videos: Methodological Aspects

Working on viral videos is, first of all, connected with teaching and learning English with film. Although some viral videos are merely collaged pictures processed by a mobile phone and iMovie or MovieMaker, the majority is professionally shot and produced. In the language classroom, proper work on film, close viewing and film analysis included, should therefore be as central as critical readings concerning the topic or gaining background knowledge about the topic. The necessity for critical reading activities frequently arises, above all, through the phenomenon of viralness itself, i.e., one video responding to another and so forth. Viralness is accompanied by intermediality, intertextuality and play on words. Wheelwright calls this the »diaphora method« (1962: 72; see also Bredella 1987: 235). In comparison to a metaphor, which is to express a similarity between something relatively well known or concretely known (the semantic vehicle), the diaphora refers to the complementary kind of semantic movement between two or more texts, which Bredella called »die unvermittelte Nebeneinanderstellung von disparaten Elementen« (Bredella 1987: 235). »Here the ›movement‹ (phora) is ›through‹ (dia) certain particulars of experience (actual or imagined) in a fresh way, producing new meaning by juxtaposition alone« (Wheelwright 1962: 70–91).[6] This means that learners negotiate and produce new meaning by juxtaposing disparate texts (videos, pictures, topics, language, etc.)

The literacy-oriented[7] methodological approach developed as a cross-language model FILM ERLEBEN, NUTZEN UND VERSTEHEN by Blell, Grünewald, Kepser and Surkamp (2016) seems to be complex enough to cover many aspects of teaching viral videos and viralness. Based on the principle that film education in all language classes should be primarily language-oriented, they define four literacy fields for experiencing, using and understanding film (see Blell, Grünewald, Kepser and Surkamp 2016: 22–42):

(A) **To explore and use language with regard to film** (FILMBEZOGEN SPRACH-LICH HANDELN)
(To use language receptively: listen, read, see and reflect; to use language productively: speak, write and act; to act multilingually: receptively and productively)

---

6   In his book *Der Fremdsprachenunterricht als Spiel der Texte und Kulturen* (2002), Hallet discusses the phenomena of intertextuality and intermediality and their value for teaching and learning.
7   'Literacy' is used synonymously with ›competence‹ in this paper.

(B) **To analyze film** (FILM ANALYSIEREN)
(To recognize, name and interpret film techniques; to acquire genre and film theoretical knowledge and use it; to recognize and interpret film as fictionally constructed; to record and understand film reception)

(C) **To contextualize film** (FILM KONTEXTUALISIEREN)
(To reflect film in our media dominated society; to recognize and interpret intertextual/-medial relations; to understand and interpret film as cultural product; to use film for inter-/transcultural learning)

(D) **To build on film** (FILM GESTALTEN)
(to draw up filmic pre-text and plan a film production; to shoot a film and use film techniques and language consciously; to revise and edit film material; to present film).

Moreover, Blell and Surkamp presume that developing subject and cross-subject film literacy requires demanding learning tasks (2016: 8–32; see Hallet and Krämer 2012 as well):

> Um Kompetenzentwicklung im Bereich filmischen Lernens auf verschiedenen Niveaustufen auszulösen und damit Outcome-Orientierung anzubahnen, benötigt ein kompetenzorientierter Filmunterricht Lernaufgaben als Steuerinstrumente. (...) Kompetenzaufgaben lösen aufgrund möglichst authentischer Lerninhalte und aufgrund ihrer Komplexität idealerweise (...) mehrdimsionale Interaktions- und Aushandlungsprozesse aus« (Blell and Surkamp 2016: 16, 17).

5 Viral Videos: Practical Teaching in the EFL Classroom

In the following section, a possible learning scenario for an advanced EFL classroom is introduced. For this scenario, a fictitious complex task is created that might easily be adapted for an authentic situation in a genuine school club or organization to constitute rich input and present process initiation. Moreover, the set task can only be accomplished as a group and requires teamwork. The teacher can provide reasonable scaffolding concerning the various literacies. Since all activities are in English, of course, the above defined literacy fields can be implicitly developed. As a result, selected features of film literacy and film production competence as well as communicative and critical literacies (reflecting on the phenomenon of viralness) are called upon.

Complex Task: Read the following e-mail that has been addressed from *The Humboldt-School English Debating Club* to your class and use the accompanying material to complete the task that is asked of you.

> Humboldt School, Viraltown, 2016-09-20
> **Be the New Spokesperson ...**
> Final Call for New Elections in The Humboldt-School English Debating Club (HSEDC)
>
> The HSEDC is urgently looking for a new spokesperson this year since the office-holding spokesperson graduated from school in July 2016. You have the unique chance to apply for this two-year position. Apply immediately. Check out the following description for more details!
>
> 1) Send us your 3-minute profile video in which you introduce yourself and your programme. Convince all the current club members and the public that you are the right spokesperson! A person on the street interview may amplify your speech.
> 2) Record your video (monologue, street interview, etc.).
> 3) Seed the actual release of your video in school with teasers, outtakes, and other fun stuff to drive interest in the video once available.
> 4) Deadline for uploading your video on the school's website: http://.www.Humboldt.school.de is 31 December 2016. This is going to be the starting point for the E-elections as well. Feel free to drive viewers to vote for your video!
> 5) The product that receives the most hits is the winner and the new spokesperson!
> 6) Attach a certificate that proves that you are the selected person in your class for an application. Good luck!
>
> If you have any further questions regarding your application, please feel free to contact the currently acting HSEDC spokesperson, Communico Bae. (communico.bae@gmx.de)

Sub-task One: Selecting the class candidates and cast the project roles

Although all ambitious students are invited to record and release their videos, the task imposes the condition that the application is based on the class's voting. Therefore, the whole group has to think of rules and criteria to find 2–3 candidates, who will be selected: personal attributes, such as enthusiasm and motivation, language (arguing) competence, and having the necessary drive. A group speaker (project organizer) can ask for candidates' applications which then will be collected and reviewed. At the same time, the project organizer can ask the shortlisted candidates' appointed referees for feedback on their performance in the interview. At the same time, all the necessary project roles have to be casted in a similar way: a crafted film team, actors for the ›person on the street interview‹, screenplay writers, and promotion team. In this step the whole class is called upon to explore and use language to start the project: reading, writing, listening and speaking. And they learn more about finding the appropriate students. (→ Literacy field (A))

Sub-task Two: How to give a good speech

Obama's speech is not only highly inspirational and about change, but students can also easily learn how one can address and make people curious: e.g. by speaking in a clear and loud voice; keeping eye contact with the audience; raising questions, using personal anecdotes to expose a problem; involving the audience using the unity word ›we‹ (leader plus teamplayer); applying catchphrases like ›Yes, We Can‹ to ingrain a takeaway phrase and, using rhetorical devices like anaphora (repetitions at the beginning) or epiphora (repetitions at the end). (→ Literacy field (A) and (B)) The following sub-task might be set:

Watch and listen to Barack Obama's famous concession speech in the New Hampshire Presidential Primary from 2008 (Youtube) and the accompanying promotion video ›Yes, We Can‹ by Will.I.Am (2008) to identify criteria to give a convincing speech. Watch a negative example as well to work out what should be avoided in a monologue. You may watch George reading his father's Christmas speech in ›The King's Speech‹ (2010). (YouTube)

Sub-task Three: Concept/ Storyboard Stage/ Filming and Editing/ Presentation

In order to stage the selected candidate for the application a worksheet might be presented including information on how to produce the video. As a first step, the learners are introduced to six main roles: producer, storyboard director, camera operator, writer, editor and actor (see Smart 2016: 10). »This is namely that they are required to reflect upon their own skills, strengths and weaknesses in order to decide which of the roles will be most suited to their profile« (Smart 2016: 10f.). Thus, the students are guided into their roles during the film production. As a second step, students e.g. watch critically Will.I.Am's ›Yes, We Can‹ once more from their role perspectives to analyze and understand how this successful clip is filmed and why it received so many hits (e.g. the clip follows a linear story, similar to Obama's speech; characters move expressively giving affirmative answers; medium and close-ups are used to zoom in on the protagonist; collage fashion and split screen multiply Obama's image, and the participating celebrities respond rhythmically to his calls). After pre-production, production and post-production, students should come together for the final presentation in class before the final release. »Here the students are required to undergo a period of reflection upon their sequence and decide what it was that they particularly enjoyed about the process, what they think they did well and what they would do differently if they had a chance to start again« (Smart 2016: 12). (Smart and his project group from my film seminar practised this stage format successfully for their own production of a visitor advertising video: ›Come to Garbsen‹.[8] (→ Literacy fields (A), (B) and (D))

Concept stage:
Medium/Close up shot showing businessman on his commute. Required features involving typical business dress. Hannover in the background.
Sound: diegetic train sounds, voiceover

Storyboard stage

Filming Stage

Presentation stage:
Shot intended to provide an example of how public transport can be used to travel between hotel and the trade fair. Shot shows face, key features of the passenger and the setting on the train, whilst maintaining the idea of movement in the background through the use of the still shot.

Fig. 2: Pre-production / production / post-production / presentation (Smart 2016: 13)

Sub-task Four: Release and make the video go viral

Task 4 of the complex task asks the students (now especially those casted for this role) to seed the actual release of the production in school (or the near neighbourhood) with teasers, outtakes, and other fun stuff to drive interest in the video once available. This might be fun and makes the students experience themselves the joint efforts to give the film a good start. Stickers with the future spokesperson's image or his/her takeaway slogan may be delivered, coffee and cake could be offered for the first bloggers online, etc. A final discussion should be organized in class to discuss the run-through promotion process of ›viral marketing‹. Not only is it important to make the students aware of this process

---

8   Smart, Eric J. (2016) ›Come to Garbsen‹ (YouTube)

in general; it is critical as well that they get a basic understanding of viral marketing, businesses and networks whose agents they all are anyway. As a preparation the introduction ›Viral President‹ from Penenberg's little book: ›Viral Loop. The Power of Pass-It-On‹ (2009) may be read, and those who have been infected by making viral films may also look into ›Video Marketing‹ (2015), an easy instruction to how to produce viral films and leverage Facebook, YouTube, etc. to build a massive audience. (→ Literacy fields (A) and (C))

6 Conclusion

The viral loop paradigm is definitely not new if we remember the Tupperware parties of the 1950s, the old Hotmail or the first Mosaic browser. In contrast, viral videos are blazing their way into the language classroom right away (see Donaghy 2015: 68). Although the format is said to be relatively ›original,‹ it actually melts together with other familiar short films like branded shorts, response films and music films. New and full of learning potential is, unquestionably, the idea of viralness. It is this viral expansion model that has propelled hits on YouTube, MySpace and Facebook to global fame and success. Due to our students' umlimited access to Web 2.0, they experience this pass-it-on phenomenon every day. Exploring the model and the philosophy of viralness behind it opens up new fields of critical thinking and discussion as well as encourages students to go viral with their own videos.

Bibliography

Print

Blell, Gabriele / Grünewald, Andreas / Kepser, Matthis / Surkamp, Carola (Hrsg.) (2016). Film in den Fächern der sprachlichen Bildung. Hohengehren, Baltmannsweile: Schneider Verlag.

Blell, Gabriele / Grünewald, Andrea / Kepser, Matthis / Surkamp, Carola (2016). Film in den Fächern Deutsch, Englisch, Französisch und Spanisch: Ein Modell zur sprach- und kulturübergreifenden Filmbildung. In: Blell, Gabriele / Grünewald, Andreas / Kepser, Matthis / Surkamp, Carola (Hrsg.) (2016). Film in den Fächern der sprachlichen Bildung. Hohengehren, Baltmannsweile: Schneider Verlag, 11–61.

Blell, Gabriele / Surkamp, Carola (2016). (Fremd-)Sprachenlernen mit Film. Theoretische Grundlagen und praxisorientierte Anwendungen für einen kompetenz- und aufgabenorientierten Fremdsprachenunterricht am Beispiel von Jim Jarmuschs *Night on Earth*. In: Gnutzmann, Claus / Königs, Frank G. / Küster, Lutz (Hrsg.) (Fremd-)Sprachenlernen mit Film. FLuL 45 (2016)1, 8–32.

Bredella, Lothar (1987). Die Struktur schüleraktivierender Methoden. Überlegungen zum Entwurf einer prozeßorientierten Literaturdidaktik. Praxis des Neusprachlichen Unterrichts 34: 3, 233–248.

Broxton, Tom/Interian, Yannet/Vaver, Jo/Wattenhofer, Mirjam (2013). Catching a Viral Video. In: Journal of Intelligent Information Systems 40 (2013), 241–259.

Donaghy, Kieran (2015). Film in Action. Teaching language using moving images. Peaslake: Delta Publishing.

Hallet, Wolfgang (2002). Fremdsprachenunterricht als Spiel der Texte und Kulturen. Intertextualität als Paradigma einer kulturwissenschaftlichen Didaktik. Trier: Wissenschaftlicher Verlag.

Hallet, Wolfgang /Krämer, Ulrich (2012)(Hrsg.). Kompetenzaufgaben im Englischunterricht. Grundlagen und Unterrichtsbeispiele. Seelze: Klett & Kallmeyer.

Hallet, Wolfgang (2012). Die komplexe Kompetenzaufgabe. In: Hallet, Wolfgang / Krämer, Ulrich (2012)(Hrsg.). Kompetenzaufgaben im Englischunterricht. Grundlagen und Unterrichtsbeispiele. Seelze: Klett & Kallmeyer, 8–19.

Henseler, Roswitha/Möller, Stefan/Surkamp, Carola (2011). Filme im Englischunterricht. Grundlagen, Methoden, Genres. Seelze: Klett & Kallmeyer.

Moore, Michael (2008). Mike's Election Guide. New York: Ground Central Publishing.

Moore, Michael (2008). Yes, We Can. Mike's ultimativer Wahlführer. München, Berlin & Zürich: Piper.

Penenberg, Adam L. (2010). Viral Loop. The Power of Pass-It-On. London: Hodder & Stoughton.

Siever, Torsten (2012). (Neue) Formen des Lehrens und Lernens im Web 2.0. In: Der Deutschunterricht 6 (2012), 16.

Smart, Eric (2016). How to maximise awareness of the work conducted during the production of film and use complex tasks to develop the related competences in English language classes. Leibniz University Hanover: Ms. (Hausarbeit).

Toffler, Alvin (1980). The Third Wave. New York: Bantam Books.

Video Marketing. How to Produce Viral Films and Leverage Facebook, YouTube, Instagram and twitter to Build a Massive Audience. Wroclaw: Entrepreneur Publishing. (2015).

Wheelwright, Philipp E. (1962). Metaphor and Reality. Bloomington: Indiana, University Press.

Internet Sources

Burgess, Jean (2008). ›All Your Chocolate Rain Are Belong to Us?‹ Viral Video, YouTube, and the Dynamics of Participatory Culture Abrufbar unter: LINK(Stand: 23.09.2016)

Leopold, Wendy (2009). YouTubing 101: Northwestern Offers Course on Viral Videos. Abrufbar unter: http://www.northwestern.edu/newscenter/stories/2009/03/viralvideo.html. (Stand: 22.09.2016)

O, Neill, Megan (2011). What Makes a Video Viral? Abrufbar unter: http://www.adweek.com/socialtimes/what-makes-a-video-viral/62414. (Stand: 22.09.2016)

O'Reilly, Tim (2005). Web 2.0: Compact Definition?Abrufbar unter: http://radar.oreilly.com/2005/10/web-20-compact-definition.html. (Stand : 22.09.2016)

TeacherTube. Abrufbar unter: http://www.teachertube.com. (Stand: 22.09.2016)
United Farm Workers. ¡History of Si se Puede! Abrufbar unter: ufw.org/_board.php?-mode=view&b_code=cc_his_research&b_no=5970&page=1&field=&key=&n=30) (Stand: 22.09.2016)
Yes, We Scan (2013). Abrufbar unter: https://www.spreadshirt.de/yes+we+s-can-A24847878. (Stand: 23.09.2016)
Wikipedia. Viral Video. Abrufbar unter: https://en.wikipedia.org/wiki/Viral_video. (Stand 22.09.2016)

Films and Viral Videos

Brené Brown on Empathy. Abrufbar unter: https://www.youtube.com/watch?v=dfB-FJVVB5xI. (Stand: 22.09.2016)
Dirksen-Thedens, Sören (2016). Scho-Ka-Kola. Boost Your Day. Abrufbar unter: https://www.youtube.com/watch?v=7dI8vU5vi_M. (student project LIH) (Stand: 22.09.2016).
Hooper, Tom (2010). The King's Speech. GB, USA, Australia (DVD).
How to Tie a Tie: The BEST Video to Tie a Double Windsor Knot. Abrufbar unter: https://www.youtube.com/watch?v=p7X7SpkkEMY. (Stand: 22.09.2016)
Little Chicks Take Their First Flight. (2015). Abrufbar unter: https://www.youtube.com/watch?v=dfBFJVVB5xI. (Stand: 22.09.2016)
One Second Everyday. Abrufbar unter: http://www.1secondeveryday.com. (Stand: 22.09.2016)
Psy's Gangman Style video. (2012). Abrufbar unter: https://www.youtube.com/watch?v=CH1XGdu-hzQ.(Stand: 22.09.2016)
Smart, Eric J. (2016). Come to Garbsen. Abrufbar unter: https://www.youtube.com/watch?v=kfloL3gUeoQ&feature=youtu.be. (Stand: 22.09.2016)
The Power of Food. Abrufbar unter: https://www.youtube.com/watch?v=20wr6x-4COmU. (Stand: 22.09.2016)
The King's Speech – Christmas Speech George V. Abrufbar unter: https://www.youtube.com/watch?v=df4jzG_zXzI. (Stand: 26.09.2016)
Volkswagen. Eyes on the Road. (2014). Abrufbar unter: https://www.youtube.com/watch?v=R22WNkYKeo8 (2014). (Stand: 22.09.2016)
Will. I. Am (2008). Yes, We Can. Abrufbar unter: https://www.youtube.com/watch?v=SsV2O4fCgjk. (Stand: 22.09.2016)
Will. I. Am (2008). We Are the Ones. Abrufbar unter: https://www.youtube.com/watch?v=ghSJsEVf0pU. (Stand: 23.09.2016)

Amazing Short Animation: »Must See / Teach« Films for the EFL Classroom

Christiane Lütge

1 Audiovisual worlds in English language education

The use of films in the EFL classroom has become very popular during the last years. School curricula mention film literacy as an important aspect of foreign language teaching and explicitly demand their integration into English lessons (Lütge 2012, Thaler 2014, Henseler / Möller / Surkamp 2011). As authentic cultural products films seem to almost ideally lend themselves to teaching purposes. Thus, the transfer into the EFL classroom does not come as a surprise and can be found in almost all school curricula. In some federal states films have even become obligatory in the final school leaving exams. According to an empirical study carried out by Thaler, two thirds of the teachers regard film as »very positive or positive« (Thaler 2007).

Among the reasons most frequently mentioned for teaching film we find aspects like the following ones: motivation, entertainment, end-of-term relaxation, language acquisition, competence development, film analysis, communicative follow-ups, book-film comparison, (inter)cultural learning, film-aesthetic aspects.

The Common European Framework of Reference for Languages (CEF) has provided a scale for watching TV and film with descriptors starting from level A2 (cf. Thaler 2014: 20). However, in spite of a growing acceptance of film in research and in the curricula, the Cinderella existence deplored by Thaler (2014: 17) must not be underrated. Two problems may be responsible here: firstly, some insecurity with regard to the goals and competences connected with the medium film. Secondly – and maybe most importantly – film is often regarded as too time-consuming and therefore the format of short films seems to be a good alternative.

2 Competence development: what is »film literacy«?

Audiovisual media in the foreign language classroom are used in the context of fostering communicative film competence or film literacy, sometimes also referred to as audio-visual literacy (cf. Thaler 2014). The latter term suggests that the combination of different sub-competences (»Kombi-Kompetenz Hörsehverstehen«, cf. Lütge 2012) is necessary. In fact, what is referred to as film literacy is much more than a simple addition of »listening plus viewing«. In a highly complex process learners must both perceive successive and simultaneous meanings (of visual and auditory channels) and integrate bottom-up and top-down processes. According to Blell and Lütge (2004), film literacy consists of the following sub-competences:

film literacy *(Filmkompetenz)*
- **perception competence** *(Wahrnehmungskompetenz)*
- **aesthetic competence** *(Filmästhetische und -kritische Kompetenz)*
- **intercultural competence** *(Interkulturelle Kompetenz)*
- **communicative competences** *(Fremdsprachliche Handlungs- und Kommunikationskompetenz)*

However, profound insights into film analysis may not be the ultimate goal of EFL lessons, which makes it important to carefully reflect the main goals for individual lessons – and the role the film is supposed to play in order to achieve these goals. Short films with their reduced plotlines and condensed narrative structures are ideal in order to foster these sub-competences separately.

3 The potential of - short - animation films

In order to gradually build up film literacy it is recommendable to start working with shorter formats rather than with long feature films right from the start. Not only does that allow for easier integration into an English lesson but it can also be helpful in order to work on particular aspects of film literacy in detail. Andrea Rössler explains the potential of short films in the following way:

> Die konzentriert-komplexe Gestaltung manifestiert sich in einer besonders hohen Dichte und Intensität filmästhetischer Mittel; dabei kommt der Montage, der Kamerabewegung, der Licht- und Musikgestaltung und nicht zuletzt der Verwendung von Metaphern und Symbolen eine besondere Bedeutung zu. Kurzfilme zeichnen sich durch eine hohe Suggestivkraft und einen hohen Überschuss an impliziter Bedeutung aus (Rössler 2009, 310 f.).

Short films can be separated into live action short films and animated short films. The latter consist of single images that are connectd through animation by various animation techniques.

Depending on the animation technique they can be grouped into the following types:

- Puppet animation,
- Claymotion,

- Lego stop motion,
- Animated cartoon,
- Paper silhouette films,
- Computer-animated films

While cultural authenticity is often seen as one of the major advantages of films in the EFL Classroom one may raise the question why animated films, which seem to be more »artificial« products, can be beneficial for language teaching. In fact – and quite counter-intuitively – this may turn out as one of the major advantages. The very fact that animated films do not feature »real« people helps pupils to maintain a certain »viewer distance«, which is sometimes all the more helpful for engaging in lively and productive communication about certain topics. Advantages of short animation films in general relate to the following aspects:

- good accessibility,
- can be used ›in between‹, can be shown several times,
- individual work possible (on computers or at home),
- clear narrative structures, not too complex plotlines (easier for summaries and while-viewing tasks),
- condensed narration with many indeterminacies (imaginative gaps), ideal for creative tasks OR guided »what will happen if ......«-scenarios,
- several films can be combined (similar topic),
- no ›real‹ people, helpful for approaching emotions (viewer distance!).

Didactic criteria for film selection would have to take the following aspects into account:

- *Film length*: Even with short films there are remarkable differences between three-minute formats and 20-minute-films that almost take up half of the lesson.
- *Adequacy of the topic*: As with every film selection process the topic must be adequate both with a view to the learners' degree of maturity, background and the respective teaching goals for the lesson. Many short fims are reduced to a single plotline and focus on a specific topic and sometimes come up with expressive or provocative solutions or »punchlines«.
- *Appropriacy of the language level*: Short films with their reduced plotlines offer generally fewer difficulties with regard to the general understanding. In many cases a decision has to be made whether a silent short film is also in line with the teaching goals.

Aspects of the teaching methodology concerning skills like listening-viewing, analysing and creating (Thaler 2014: 40) need to be considered for short films as well. The relationship between sound and image (congruence or contradiction) needs to be taken into account in order to decide about adequate pre-, while- and post-viewing activities. Short films, which can be watched several times, have the advantage that they need not be »disturbed« too much – or too often – with extensive while-watching activities, which will leave more time and opportunity for experiencing the emotional or aesthetic appeal of a film. Announcing the film length is generally helpful in order to structure the viewing process and the concentration span. Short animation films can be used for younger learners and open up various opportunities for different grades.

4 Must-see / teach films? ... and where to find them

Considering the aforementioned selection criteria the following grids provide suggestions for short animation films grouped together according to film length, level and the question whether or not there is some English language input.

Time	Level
Short animation films – up to 5 minutes	**Short animation films – beginners**
1. John and Karen 2. Taking Pictures 3. The Piano	1. The Present 2. The Scarecrow 3. Thought of You
Short animation films – 5–10 minutes	**Short animation films – intermediate learners**
1. Lost Property 2. Fear of flying 3. Feast	1. Obvious to you. Amazing to others. 2. Sidewalk 3. The Gift
Short animation films – 10–20 minutes	**Short animation films – advanced learners**
1. The Violin 2. Caldera 3. The Origin of Creatures	1. Serial Taxi 2. Blinky 3. The Man Who Planted Trees

Table 1: Suggestions for short films (time / level)

English language input	Silent movie
The cat came back (beginners) **Alarm** (beginners/intermdediate) **The Present** (pre-intermediate/intermediate) **John and Karen** (intermediate) **The Meaning of Life** (advanced) **Lily and Jim** (advanced) **Everything will be okay** (advanced) **Junk** (advanced)	**Kiwi!** (beginners) **Oktapodi** (intermediate) **Silent, a short film** (intermediate to advanced) **Father and Daughter** (advanced) **Endless** (advanced) (winner bronze world medal, New York festivals 2013) **Drawn** (advanced) (winner gold medal, New York festivals 2013) **Balance** (advanced) (Academy Award 1989)

Table 2: Short animation films (language)

Short animation films

A list of Oscar nominated short films
http://www.imdb.com/find?ref_=nv_sr_fn&q=short+animated+films&s=all

Lesson suggestions using film clips and short animation
http://moviesegmentstoassessgrammargoals.blogspot.de/

Collection of stop animation and tutorials
http://www.stopmotionanimation.com

Regular updates of new short animations
https://www.shortoftheweek.com/channels/animation/

Webpage with numerous short films
http://www.filmsshort.com/genre/Animated-Short-Films-1.html

A collection of short films and video clips, with subtitles, quizzes and classroom materials.
https://www.englishclub.com/esl-videos/

More short (animation) films and classroom materials
http://www.multimedia-english.com/videos/section/official-1/tag/short-film-88

Must-see short animation films
http://listverse.com/2012/12/16/10-must-see-animated-short-films/

Table. 3: List of useful websites for short animation films

5 Challenging topics in animated short films

One of the advantages of short animation film is their potential for dealing with challenging topics like pain, sorrow, death, human suffering through the experience of animated characters, which creates a special atmosphere. Ranging somewhere between unrealistic cartoon settings and imagined dreamworld realities, animation formats create a distance between the viewer and the film's protagonists and at the same time make it possible to encounter these filmic formats much more openly. Expressing the inexpressible in audiovisions and still keeping the viewer in a safe distance is a big advantage of short animation films. The film *Endless* (3:07 minutes), winner of the Bronze World Medal at the New York Festivals 2013, is an impressive example. It displays a suicide scene of a young woman and the attempt of a man who comes too late to rescue her. Music and images are carefully composed so as to lead the viewer into the mood of the story. Despite its sinister plot this film is immensely impressive and due to its careful composition of images never too depressing. It offers possibilities for sensitive approaches to one of the most difficult topics.

Similarly, *Father and Daughter* (9:22 minutes) – described as »a wordless poem« – and the winner of an Academy Award (category best short film, animation) in 2000, has a remarkable capacity to move an audience. The story of a father and a daughter and their tearful and mysterious goodbye followed by years of waiting and longing on the part of the daughter develops into an impressive tale about life. As a silent movie it is again the artistic composition of music and images which evokes a touching atmosphere stimulating many communicative impulses.

Not quite as difficult as these examples but also challenging in a different way are many of the animated short films by Don Hertzfeldt. *Lily and Jim* (13 minutes), for which the director single-handedly animated over 10,000 drawings, tells the amusing story of the challenging situation of a blind date of a nervous young couple, yet another great example for classroom use. The simplification – and thus alienation – of the characters into stick figures causes an estrangement effect that helps the story to unfold. Jim and Lily but also other Hertzfeldt animation films (like *World of Tomorrow* or *Meaning of Life*) are excellent for classroom use.

6 »Do it yourself« approaches: animate and motivate?

Animation films can easily be produced by the pupils themselves. Mobile phones can be used for animating lego brick or playmobil versions. Special websites offer tutorials for animating photos, pictures and single clips. »Quick as a brick«

is a suggestion by Möller/Plum (2011) using Windows moviemaker in order to produce stop-motion-films. Cooperative projects that can be initiated on a topic like bullying via paper clips produced with a scanner offer various scenarios for creative classroom work (Stritzelberger 2011a). Five steps towards producing a film in an EFL Classroom have been put forward by Brickart, Haack and Menzel (2011). Many English lessons focus on the topic of »What I like doing«. What Ingrid Stritzelberger (2011b) suggests here lies at the heart of every short animation film, the production of an animation flip book. The full potential of this amazing audiovisual format of short animation films has not yet been fully acknowledged in EFL teaching.

Bibliography

Print

Blell, Gabriele and Christiane Lütge. 2004. »Sehen, Hören, Verstehen und Handeln: Filme im Fremdsprachenunterricht«. *Praxis Fremdsprachenunterricht* 6. 402–405, 445.
Brickart, Dario, Adrian Haack and Moritz Menzel. 2011. »Five Steps Towards a Successful Movie. Einen eigenen Film im Unterricht produzieren«. *Der Fremdsprachliche Unterricht Englisch* 112/113 (45): 10–17.
Henseler, Roswitha, Stefan Möller, and Carola Surkamp. 2011. *Filme im Englischunterricht. Grundlagen, Methoden, Genres.* Seelze: Kallmeyer.
Henseler, Roswitha, Stefan Möller, and Carola Surkamp. 2011. »Filme verstehen, Filme drehen«. *Der Fremdsprachliche Unterricht Englisch 112/113 (45):* 2–17.
Lütge, Christiane. 2012. *Mit Filmen Englisch unterrichten.* Berlin: Cornelsen.
Mainda, Dorothee and Kati Struckmeyer. 2011. »Who Would Like to Be an Actor. Handyclips im Englischunterricht«. *Der Fremdsprachliche Unterricht Englisch* 112/113 (45): 1–3.
Möller, Stefan and Fabian Plum. 2011. »Quick as a Brick. Stop-Motion-Filme: einen Brickfilm mit Windows Moviemaker herstellen« *Der Fremdsprachliche Unterricht Englisch* 112/113 (45): 8–9.
Rössler, Andrea. 2009. »Überraschende Begegnung der kurzen Art: Zum Einsatz von Kurzspielfilmen im Fremdsprachenunterreicht«. *Filme im Fremdsprachenunterricht.* Ed. Eva Leitzke-Ungerer. Stuttgart: ibidem Verlag. 309–321.
Stritzelberger, Ingrid. 2011a. »The Bullied Paper Clip. Einen Trickfilm am Scanner zum Thema »Mobbing« erstellen. *Der Fremdsprachliche Unterricht Englisch* 112/113 (45): 4–6.
Stritzelberger, Ingrid. 2011b. »What I Like Doing. Sich selbst präsentieren in einem Animation Flip Book«. *Der Fremdsprachliche Unterricht Englisch* 112/113 (45): 7.
Thaler, Engelbert. 2014. *Teaching English with Films.* Paderborn [u.a.]: Schöningh.

Short films

Alarm. 2009. Dir. Mu-hyun Jang.
Apollo. 2010. Dir. Felix Gönnert.
Balance. 1989. Dir. Christoph Lauenstein and Wolfgang Lauenstein.
Blinky. 2012. Dir. Ruairi Robinson.
Caldera. 2012. Dir. Evan Viera.
Drawn. 2015. Dir. Darcie Thompson.
Everything will be okay. 2006. Dir. Don Hertzfeldt.
Father and Daughter. 2000. Dir. Michaël Dudok de Wit.
Fear of flying. 2013. Dir. Conor Finnegan.
Feast. 2014. Dir. Patrick Osborne.
John und Karen. 2007. Dir. Matthew Walker.
Junk. 2011. Dir. Kirk Hendry.
Kiwi! 2006. Dir. Dony Permedi.
Lily and Jim. 1997. Dir. Don Hertzfeldt.
Lost Property. 2014. Dir. Åsa Lucander.
Obvious to you. Amazing to others. 2011. Derek Sivers.
Oktapodi. 2007. Dir. Julien Bocabeille, François-Xavier Chanioux, Olivier Delabarre, Thierry, Marchand, Quentin Marmier, Emud Mokhberi. Gobelins l'école de l'image.
Serial Taxi. 2013. Dir. Paolo Cogliati.
Sidewalk. 2013. Dir. Celia Bullwinkel.
Silent, a short film. 2014. Dolby Laboratories.
Taking Pictures. 2015. Dir. Simon. Taylor.
The Origin of Creatures. 2010. Dir. Floris Kaayk.
The Present. 2014. Dir. Jacob Frey.
The Piano. 2012. Dir. Aidan Gibbons.
The Scarecrow. 2013. Dir. Brandon Oldenburg, Limbert Fabian.
The Violin. 2015. Dir. Ervin Han.
Thought of You. 2010. Dir. Ryan Woodward.
The Gift. 2016. MARZA Movie Pipeline for Unity
The Man Who Planted Trees. 1987. Dir. Frédéric Back
The cat came back. 1988. Dir. Cordell Barker.
The Meaning of Life. 2005. Dir. Don Hertzfeldt.

Exposing Learners to Authentic Language in Short Video Clips in the EFL Classroom

Matthias Hutz

1 Using authentic videos in the EFL classroom

The question of authenticity in the EFL classroom has been debated for a long time. Classroom materials have often been criticized for not reflecting real language use and for being artificial. In reaction to this, a great passion for authentic materials, such as films, radio broadcasts, magazines or newspaper clippings, etc. developed (e.g. Scrivener 2011: 127) in order to expose learners to examples of spoken and written discourse by native speakers.

However, even nowadays there are still many complaints about the lack of authenticity and the artificiality of coursebook materials and classroom discourse. The simplified texts used in coursebooks are to a large extent still designed and adapted for specific groups of language learners. In addition, they often have a ›hidden agenda‹, i.e. they sometimes serve the purpose of introducing specific grammatical items by including high quantities of specific target language items.

Traditionally, authentic materials have been defined »as those which have been produced for purposes other than to teach language« (Nunan 1988: 9). Therefore, an authentic text »is a stretch of real language, produced by a real speaker or writer for a real audience and designed to convey a real message of some sort« (Morrow 1977: 13). Authenticity in the classroom, however, can occur in different shapes. According to Brown and Menasche (2006), five different levels of input authenticity can be distinguished:

a. Genuine input authenticity, i.e. materials which were not produced for teaching purposes, but for real-life communicative purposes (e.g. films or newspapers).
b. Altered input authenticity, i.e. original materials which are presented with specific aids for learners (e.g. annotated stories or newspaper articles).
c. Adapted input authenticity, i.e. texts which were created for a real-life purpose, but which were simplified lexically or syntactically for learning purposes (e.g. special readers for EFL classes).

d. Simulated input authenticity, i.e. materials that were specifically created for learners, but which have an appearance similar to authentic materials (e.g. school timetables).
e. Inauthenticity, i.e. materials that were specifically designed for language learners and for learning purposes (e.g. grammar exercises).

One of the best ways to expose learners to genuine input and to authentic spoken language is to watch English films and video clips. Films have numerous general advantages, of course (for an overview see, for instance, Thaler 2014: 19f. or Donaghy 2015), including, for instance, personal relevance for learners and their popularity. Another vital benefit of using films is that they are »cultural documents« (Donaghy 2015: 19) and provide »a window into culture« (Sherman 2003: 12). They can communicate cultural values, customs and attitudes as well as expose learners to specific cultural or social phenomena (e.g. gender roles) or to various aspects of everyday life. By doing this, they can increase learners' intercultural understanding and competence (Leitzke-Ungerer 2009: 15).

Short video clips (e.g. news, weather reports, commercials, comedy sketches, interviews, trailers), in particular, have proved to be a very valuable source for learners since short films are brief, accessible and tell stories that learners can understand (cf. Thaler 2014: 21, Donaghy 2015: 25, Rössler 2009). They can therefore be easily integrated into a single lesson. Since they typically focus on a single idea as well and often deal with contemporary subjects and issues, they are ideal prompts for oral communication and for conversational activities in the classroom (Donaghy 2015: 25). In addition, ›shorties‹ such as animated lectures, viral shorts, music clips, comedy sketches, interviews or commercials provide learners with excellent models of the target language (Lonergan 1984: 86). Film-sharing sites such as YouTube provide an overwhelming abundance of videos and films which are between two and five minutes long and are therefore ideal when class time is limited.

2 Exposing Learners to real-life language and interaction through »shorties«

Films also provide a great source of natural language use and ›real-life‹ communication which helps them see the foreign language used in ›real‹ situations outside the classroom (Donaghy 2015: 18f.; Baral 2009: 2; Lennon 2002: 35). Films usually represent a kind of language which students may face in an English-speaking environment, including numerous features of spoken language discourse (e.g. colloquial language, hedges, fillers) and a natural flow of speech (Tomlinson 2003: 5; Hohmann 1996: 7). This is important since, as Jane Sherman (2003: 14) states, »students need such exposure because to learn to speak to people they must see and hear people speaking to each other«. If access to the English-speaking world is mainly confined to the classroom, perhaps only film and television can provide them with this real-life language input.

In addition to this, learners can become familiar with various characteristics of interactive language. Learners can, for example, gain insights into the ways conversations are structured, certain speech acts (e.g. requests, apologies or complaints) are performed or turn-taking is organized. In short, the learners' sociolinguistic and pragmatic competence can be increased through films. In this way, learners may eventually be challenged to interact naturally in the language as well.

It is often difficult to offer a wide range of interactive language in the classroom. Simulated materials and inauthentic dialogues in coursebooks are not necessarily the best way to help students cope with the language they will experience outside the classroom. Instead, learners »need extensive exposure to realistic interaction as wide-range models for their own speech« (Sherman 2003: 14). Otherwise learners may not be able to produce natural spoken English and instead resort to scholastic language, distorted idioms and have a limited repertoire of functional language and colloquial expressions (Sherman 2003: 14).

In particular, authentic spoken language is still largely neglected in the classroom. Clearly enunciated teacher talk and the use of scripted dialogues in textbooks and CDs with recordings by actors often lead to the establishment of ›EFL-speak‹ (Lewis 2008: 97) while at the same time characteristic features of spoken discourse, such as high-frequency »lexical chunks«, phrasal verbs and other idiomatic expressions are neglected.

The main reason for the neglect of authentic spoken language is that teachers and textbook authors often consider this input to be too complex for learners, in particular for beginners and intermediate learners. It is often felt that there is »no control of language in the applied linguistics sense of course design« (Lonergan 1984: 81). As a result of this, there is a great deal of ›restricted exposure‹, i.e. texts which are recognizably simplified and specifically adapted to match the competence of the learners and to make them more accessible (Scrivener 2011: 127).

However, this seemingly ›learner-friendly‹ approach may, in fact, do learners »a great disservice« (Schmitt 2016: 81) and perhaps eventually result in a rude awakening for learners as Celce-Murcia et al. (2010: 175) note:

»When confronted by authentic native-speaker discourse, learners are often initially frustrated by issues such as the rapidity of native-speaker speech and by their inability to decipher word boundaries and/or recognize words or phrases.«

It goes without saying that it can be a very motivating experience for learners if they have the feeling that they can ›conquer‹ an authentic movie or video clip. However, this is often easier said than done when learners and teachers are confronted with the complexity of natural language use. Dealing with genuine input and, in particular, with spoken discourse has proved to be one of the most challenging areas in foreign language teaching. Therefore, in the next chapter some of the main difficulties will be presented and discussed.

3 What makes videos difficult to understand: Characteristics of authentic language

Almost all language learners, in particular beginners and lower-intermediate learners, have had this experience: Watching a clip or movie which is beyond one's linguistic proficiency can be an extremely frustrating experience. Learners often get lost after a few minutes when they have to cope with a movie without subtitles. They are forced to rely on the visual clues, including non-verbal and paraverbal cues, but this does not always compensate for the linguistic deficits.

A good example of this is the comedy sketch »Voice recognition elevator« (https://www.youtube.com/watch?v=5FFRoYhTJQQ) from »Burnistoun«, a Scottish comedy sketch show broadcast by BBC Scotland. In this hilarious episode, two Scottish people battle with a voice-activated lift. They want to get to the 11th floor, but the elevator fails to recognize their pronunciation of »eleven« due to their Scottish accent. This is the beginning of the transcript:

Iain:	Where's the buttons?	
Rob:	No, no, they've installed voice recognition in this lift. I've heard about this.	
Iain:	Voice recognition technology? In a lift? In Scotland? You ever tried voice recognition technology?	
Rob:	No.	
Iain:	They don't do Scottish accents.	
Rob:	Eleven!	
Voice:	Could you please repeat that?	
Rob:	Eleven.	
Rob:	Eleven. Eleven.	
Iain:	Eleven.	
Voice:	Could you please repeat that?	

Rob:	Eleven!
Iain:	Whose idea was this? You need to try an American accent: Eleven. Eleven.
Rob:	That sounds Irish, not American.
Iain:	Doesn't it? Eleven.
Rob:	Where in America is that? Dublin?
Iain:	I'm sorry, could you please repeat that?
Rob:	Try an English accent, alright? Eleven! Eleven!
Iain:	Are you from the same part in England as Dick van Dyke?
Rob:	Let's hear yours then, smartass!
Voice:	Please speak slowly and clearly.
Rob:	Smartass!
Iain:	Eleven. If you don't understand our lingo, away back home to your own country!

The transcript may give the impression that this dialogue could be easily understood by learners, but when watching this sketch, learners – even very advanced ones – are faced with numerous difficulties which might eventually hinder comprehension. For instance, if learners are not familiar with Scottish English, they may face phonological problems (e.g. pronunciation of diphthongs), lexical problems (e.g. »aye«) as well as problems due to different intonation patterns. The speakers talk very fast and use contractions (»wanna«) as well as informal register (»lingo«, »smartass«). Furthermore, potential general lexical problems (»pathetic«, »voice recognition«) and grammatical problems (e.g. elliptic sentences such as »You ever tried voice recognition technology?«) and content-related problems (Who is ›Dick van Dyke‹?) may impair comprehension as well.

Generally speaking, spoken language in conversations tends to be rather ›messy‹. In particular, it is assumed that the following factors contribute to the difficulties when faced with authentic language in videos (cf. also Schmitt 2016: 81; Cauldwell 2013; Sherman 2003: 15; Thaler 1999: 151):

a. Rate of speed
   Spontaneous, unscripted language by native speakers tends to be much faster than classroom discourse or scripted dialogues – this typically leads to high verbal density which makes it harder to process the input.
b. Characteristics of spoken discourse
   Typical features of spoken discourse include, for instance, incomplete sentences, false starts, elliptic constructions and overlapping when multiple

speakers are talking at the same time. If learners are mainly confronted with well-formed sentences in written discourse, this may lead to problems. Phenomena of connected speech such as the assimilation of sound segments, elision and liaison may lead to what Cauldwell (2013: 18) has referred to as ›acoustic blur‹.

c. Different varieties of English
Learners are often not familiar with regional accents and/or lesser known international varieties of English (Hutz 2015). It is also a well-known fact that Received Pronunciation is not as widely spread as people generally think it is.

d. Register
Spoken discourse is often associated with informal and colloquial expressions that learners are often unfamiliar with.

e. Background noises
Natural background noises (e.g. music, traffic) can be distracting for learners and may also represent an additional hindrance for comprehension.

It is generally helpful to adopt a realistic perspective with regard to the linguistic and content-related complexities of authentic videos. Ignoring the difficulties which may result from the exposure to authentic language may only lead to frustration, in particular since it is not unusual that many of the factors mentioned above may be found in combination when watching authentic videos.

However, this does not mean that learners should not be exposed to authentic videos at all since the advantages of working with natural discourse clearly outweigh the disadvantages. Learners need to become familiar with different accents and need to develop strategies to cope with videos.

The following part therefore deals with numerous strategies how teachers may help learners to facilitate the comprehension process when faced with authentic language in videos.

4 How to improve language comprehension: Implications for the classroom

The following strategies may help to reduce difficulties for learners:

a) Choosing appropriate videos

- Choosing videos with an adequate linguistic level
 The degree of linguistic complexity of videos may vary considerably. For beginners, it might not be the best idea to choose a video in which lots of speakers using a rural accent are talking simultaneously about a special topic; clearly enunciated speech usually facilitates comprehension.

- Choosing videos with relevant and interesting topics for learners
  The more learners are familiar with the topics the easier comprehension will be for them. As a teacher, one should also take the students' viewing habits into account. Letting learners choose videos they are interested in (e.g. comedy sketches) can be a helpful strategy, too.
- Selecting videos which offer visual clues
  Videos with unambiguous action, clear conventional story lines and a close connection between speech and action typically aid comprehension (Sherman 2003: 15).

b) Focusing on global understanding

EFL learners sometimes underestimate their listening ability and »attempt to catch every word they hear and when they miss words, they believe they cannot understand the main ideas« (Larimer 1999: 9). They primarily rely on bottom-up strategies, focusing on pronunciation, vocabulary and grammar. With a high rate of speed, this process may result in a feeling of being lost and they switch off when watching authentic videos.

Instead, it is important to encourage learners to focus on global understanding rather than on detailed comprehension, i.e. they should not adopt a »having-to-understand-everything-attitude« (Thaler 2014: 29). This also implies that they are encouraged to bridge lexical gaps, to anticipate content and »to listen with their mind« (Larimer 1999: 4), i.e. to make intelligent guesswork. In other words, learners need to rely more on top-down processing by utilizing their background knowledge (e.g. genre knowledge or world knowledge). In this way they will also gain greater autonomy.

The following table shows some of the aspects with regard to data-driven (= bottom-up) processing and knowledge-driven (= top-down) processing (cf. also Sherman 2003: 15 f. and Larimer 1998: 8):

	Bottom-up	Top-down
»Difficult for learners«	• speakers speak too fast • high verbal density • multiple speakers at the same time • high degree of naturalism in the speech: e.g. casual, informal, unscripted speech, idiomatic expressions • unknown words, jargon and special terminology • features of spoken language (e.g. assimilation, ellipsis, non-standard grammatical forms) • strong regional accents or elaborated styles • loud soundtracks and background noise	• learners are not familiar with the topic • learners are not familiar with the film genre and storylines • words do not match the action (e.g. irony)
»Easy for learners«	• high degree of visual support • use of subtitles • speakers use easy, common vocabulary • clearly enunciated speech in standard accents	• learners are familiar with the general topic • conventional storylines, unambiguous action • close connection between speech and action • films match the learners' viewing habits

Table 1: Aspects of difficulty

c) Using specific viewing techniques and subtitles

Repeated viewings, but also specific viewing techniques such as »silent viewing« (sound off, vision on), »blind listening« (sound on, vision off) or »freeze frame« (freezing an image for a short period so that learners can try to predict how the story might continue) may help learners to deal with some of the difficulties caused by real-life communication in videos.

If available, listening comprehension may also be facilitated by using English subtitles. This certainly improves comprehension, but typically promotes reading skills rather than listening skills since »the eye is more powerful than the ear« (Sherman 2003: 16). Subtitles may also be used temporarily to »tune into« a difficult film (Thaler 2008: 181).

d) Tasks and activities

As far as reading, listening and viewing are concerned the PWP (pre – while – post)-model has become a common sequence in the EFL classroom (Thaler 2014: 30).

Pre-viewing activities may be used to activate the learners' pre-knowledge, to introduce the topic and to motivate the learners. While-viewing activities primarily facilitate comprehension by focusing on global understanding and on specific details. Post-viewing activities finally serve to help learners to analyse the content and to deepen their understanding of the subject-matter. This is also the phase where speaking and writing skills can be practised in creative tasks such as writing a script with a different ending or interviewing some of the characters.

In all three phases samples of naturalistic conversational data that are provided by video clips can be analysed. A potential task might be, for instance, to ask learners to find expressions and phrases which express certain speech acts such as »well-wishing«, »disagreeing« or »parting« (Sherman 2003: 176). For beginners, a list with expressions (e.g. »have a good day«, »have a great time«, »enjoy yourself«, »bless you«, »good luck«) might be provided before viewing. Some of the expressions might occur in the clip, while others do not.

In the final section, three activities (adapted from Donaghy 2015) have been selected to show how authentic language can be dealt with in the classroom. The purpose of the activities, which can be used during the pre-viewing or while-viewing stage, is to reduce the difficulties for learners when confronted with real-life communication and at the same time to make learners aware of useful idiomatic expressions which are common in spoken discourse. In each case a specific film clip has been chosen to illustrate the activity.

4.1 Film bingo: Listening for lexical chunks

Objective:
To listen for common idiomatic expressions (»lexical chunks«) used in a film clip

Procedure:
The teacher presents or dictates a number of common expressions and phrases to learners. About half of the expressions occur in the film, but the other half does not. The learners are told that they will hear some of the expressions, but not all of them and that they have to tick those they hear. When the last item on the list has been ticked off, the learners shout »bingo«. After this while-viewing activity the lexical chunks can be paraphrased and explained

and the learners can be encouraged to use the idioms in a slightly different context in order to practise them.

Example: Football jargon
Listening to an English commentary of a sports event can be a great challenge, even for very advanced learners. The rate of speech is high and the commentary often contains a wide range of phenomena associated with spoken discourse (e.g. informal expressions and connected speech). In addition to this, numerous special terms and phrases are used and there is a great deal of background noise as well. In the following »football bingo« activity the learners have to mark the »chunks« they hear. The examples are taken from a commentary during the famous semi-final match between Brazil and Germany (1-7) which took place during the World Cup in 2014.

(Source: https://www.youtube.com/watch?v=pyaVuA1D17U)

Football bingo
Tick off the the ten phrases and expressions you hear in the following sports commentary from the World Cup Final 2014 (Brazil vs. Germany 1–7). Shout ›bingo‹ when you have heard all of them! Afterwards, try to explain five of the phrases in your own words.

- ☐ Kick and rush
- ☐ To disallow a goal
- ☐ What a finish!
- ☐ A tap-in
- ☐ All-time world cup goal scorer
- ☐ Beautiful timing
- ☐ Sending off a player

- ☐ A brilliant save
- ☐ A right winger
- ☐ A beautiful challenge
- ☐ A killer pass
- ☐ A wide shot
- ☐ Taking a dive
- ☐ To be two down

4.2 Scrambled texts

Objective:
To make the learners familiar with lexical phrases and to activate their background knowledge in a pre-viewing activity.

Procedure:
Several extracts of spoken language from a video can be presented to learners in such a way that they are not in a chronological order. In small groups, they are asked to put the jumbled pieces in the correct order and to justify their decision. They can also be asked to predict what the film clip might be about. Afterwards the film is shown and the groups can check whether they sequenced the extracts correctly.

Example: A brief history of the United States
The introductory scene from Michael Moore's well-known film »Bowling for Columbine« contains an animated »brief history« of the USA in just a little more than three minutes. This cartoon sequence, which is spoken very fast and with a strong American accent, also contains numerous informal expressions and common discourse markers (e.g. »well, just in the nick of time«, »to freak out«). In order to reduce the linguistic complexity, several sentences can be extracted from the video and jumbled up, for example:
- And everyone lived happily ever after.
- Once upon a time there were these people in Europe called Pilgrims and they were afraid of being persecuted. So they all got on a boat and sailed to the New World where they wouldn't have to be scared ever again.
- Well, just in the nick of time came Samuel Colt who in 1836 invented the first weapon ever that could be fired over and over without having to reload.
- The white people back then were also afraid of doing any work. So they went to Africa, kidnapped thousands of black people, brought them back to America and forced them to work very hard for no money.
- Well you can pretty much guess what came next. The slaves started rebelling, there were riots and all their masters' heads got chopped off. And when white people heard of this they were freaking out and going: ›I wanna live. Don't kill me big, black man‹.
- But as soon as they arrived they were greeted by savages and they got scared all over again. So they killed them all. Now you'd think wiping out a race of people would calm them down but no, instead, they started getting frightened of each other.

The learners have to re-arrange the sequence in such a way that the chronological order is restored. They may also guess what the short video could be about.

Afterwards the transcript may be used to discuss the colloquial expressions found in the text. A further post-viewing activity might be to transform the text into a more formal register to make learners aware of differences between individual registers.

4.3 Dialogue dictogloss

Objective:
To reconstruct an authentic dialogue and to perform it

Procedure:
The teacher selects a video or a film scene which contains an interesting conversation among several people. Quite often, this works well with comedy sketches. During the first viewing the film is shown with vision and sound on. During the second viewing several groups of learners are requested to concentrate on what specific characters are saying and to write down key words and short phrases. During a groupwork session the groups now try to reconstruct the dialogue as closely as possible.

Afterwards they can try to perform the same sketch using as many phrases as possible from the clip. For advanced learners the video can also be played again with the sound off while they are performing the roleplay.

Example: Computer says no (Little Britain)
(Source: https://www.youtube.com/watch?v=0n_Ty_72Qds)

Little Britain was a very popular sketch show broadcast on BBC. One of the characters in several episodes is a very rude and grumpy receptionist in a hospital who refuses to cooperate with patients. In this sketch a mother wants to make an appointment for her daughter to have her tonsils removed, but her daughter is asked to do a hip replacement instead. The video is 2:30 long and contains numerous common phrases needed to fill out forms and to provide personal data. Since the rate of speech is rather slow, a reconstruction of the conversation can be accomplished in groupwork. Later on, learners may write and perform their own sketches based on the general pattern of the sketch and some of the expressions.

5 Conclusion

Helping learners to ›conquer‹ real-life communication is one of the most challenging tasks in the classroom. Since watching films is an integral part of learners' lives and and since having access to English films and television series is often a key motivation for many of them, we should try to find ways to help them cope with the enormous complexities of natural discourse. The exploration of such authentic discourse which was not specifically designed for learners may ultimately promote the learners' ability to interact naturally in the English language, too.

Bibliography

Baral, Lekh N. (2009): An Investigation of Authenticity in a Nepalese Secondary ESL Textbook and its Supplementation. In: Journal of NELTA 14 (1–2), 1–13.

Bocanegra-Valle, Ana (2010): Evaluating and Designing Materials for the ESP Classroom. In: Miguel F. Ruiz-Garrido / Palmer-Silveira, Juan C./Fortanet-Gómez, Inmaculada (eds.). English for Professional and Academic Purposes. Amsterdam; New York: Rodopi, 143–167.

Breen, Michael P. (1985): Authenticity in the Language Classroom. In: Applied Linguistics 6 (1), 60–70.

Brown, Steve / Menasche, Lionel (2006): Defining Authenticity. http://class.ysu.edu/~english/faculty/brown/personal/BrownMenasche.doc

Cauldwell, Richard (2013). Phonology for Listening: Teaching the Stream of Speech. Birmingham: Speech in Action.

Celce-Murica, Marianne / Brinton, Donna M./Goodwin, Janet M./Griner, Barry (eds.) (²2010). Teaching Pronunciation: A Course Book and Reference Guide. Cambridge: Cambridge University Press.

Donaghy, Kieran (2015). Film in Action: Teaching Language Using Moving Images. Peaslake, Surrey: Delta Publishing.

Gilmore, Alex (2007). Authentic Materials and Authenticity in the EFL Classroom. In: Language Teaching 40 (2), 97–118.

Hutz, Matthias (2015). English around the World – Varietäten des Englischen erforschen. In: Der Fremdsprachliche Unterricht 134, 40–47.

Hohmann, Heinz-Otto (1996). Authentische Texte beim Spracherwerb – Reiz und Risiko. In: Zielsprache Englisch 26 (3), 7–8.

Larimer, Ruth E./Schleicher, Leigh (eds.) (1999). New Ways in Using Authentic Materials in the Classroom. New Ways in TESOL Series II: Innovative Classroom Techniques. Alexandria, VA: Teachers of English to Speakers of Other Languages (TESOL).

Lee, Winnie Yuk-Chun (1995). Authenticity Revisited: Text Authenticity and Learner Authenticity. In: ELT Journal 49 (4), 323–328.

Lennon, Paul (2002). Authentische Texte im Grammatikunterricht. Wie Schüler und Lehrer gemeinsam das Sprachsystem neu entdecken können. In: Praxis des neusprachlichen Unterrichts 49 (3), 227–236.

Leitzke-Ungerer, Eva (2009). Film im Fremdsprachenunterricht: Herausforderungen, Chancen, Ziele. In: Leitzke-Ungerer, Eva (Hrsg.). Film im Fremdsprachenunterricht: Literarische Stoffe, interkulturelle Ziele, mediale Wirkung. Stuttgart: ibidem-Verlag, 11–32.

Lewis, Michael (2008). The Lexical Approach: The State of ELT and a Way Forward. North Way, Andover: Heinle.

Lonergan, Jack (1984). Video in Language Teaching. Cambridge: Cambridge University Press.

Morrow, Keith (1977). Authentic Texts in ESP. In: Holden, Susan (ed.). English for Specific Purposes. London: Modern English Publications.

Newby, David (2000): Authenticity. In: Fenner, Anne-Brit & Newby David (eds.). Approaches to Materials Design in European Textbooks: Implementing Principles of Authenticity, Learner Autonomy, Cultural Awareness. Strasbourg: European Centre for Modern Languages, 16–23.

Nunan, David (1988): The Learner-Centred Curriculum. A Study in Second Language Teaching. Cambridge: Cambridge University Press.

Peacock, Matthew (1997): The Effect of Authentic Materials on the Motivation of EFL Learners. In: ELT Journal 51 (2), 144–156.

Rössler, Andrea (2009). Überraschende Begegnungen der kurzen Art: Zum Einsatz von Kurzspielfilmen im Fremdsprachenunterricht. In: Leitzke-Ungerer, Eva (Hrsg.). Film im Fremdsprachenunterricht: Literarische Stoffe, interkulturelle Ziele, mediale Wirkung. Stuttgart: ibidem-Verlag, 309–326.

Scrivener, Jim (^{3}2011). Learning Teaching: The Essential Guide to English Language Teaching. Oxford: Macmillan.

Sherman, Jane (2003). Using Authentic Video in the Language Classroom. Cambridge: Cambridge University Press.

Schmitt, Holger (2016). Teaching English Pronunciation: A Textbook for the German-speaking Countries. Heidelberg: Universitätsverlag Winter.

Schmitt-Egner, Diana (2007). Authentic Texts and Real-World Activities in the Classroom. An Approach to Improving English Language Skills. Norderstedt: Books on Deman.

Thaler, Engelbert (1999). Musikvideoclips im Englischunterricht: Phänomenologie, Legitimität, Didaktik und Methodik eines neuen Mediums. München: Langenscheidt-Longman.

Thaler, Engelbert (2008). Teaching English Literature. Paderborn: UTB Schöningh.

Thaler, Engelbert (2014). Teaching English with Films. Paderborn: UTB Schöningh.

Thornbury, Scott (2006). How to Teach Speaking. Oxford: Oxford University Press.

Tomlinson, Brian (2003). Introduction: Are Materials Developing? In: Brian Tomlinson (ed.). Developing Materials for Language Teaching. London, New York: Continuum, 1–14.

Dumb Ways to Die – a Morbid But Fun Way to Learn with a *Shorty*

Christoph Werth

Have you ever heard about the so-called *Darwin Award*? Let me assure you, your pupils have. And this unfortunately holds true despite the fact that the award in question literally is about the dumbest way to die (or at least to sterilize yourself) in real life. It is unofficial, tongue-in-cheek and granted online. And yes, the winner very often is not among the living any more to accept the trophy. Disturbing! ... but yet part of real life as modern teenagers encounter it.[1]

This article will not take into consideration this former (morbid and rather macabre) competition at all but it will – to some extent – use the children's *Schadenfreude* to instigate learning processes concerning vocabulary, grammar and also to make them reflect this latter fascination and their attitudes towards a topic as serious as *death* and *dying*. However, there is a humorous way to approach this topic, which – even at its worst – develops a very British and »fun« perspective on stupid accidents and their lethal consequences. Even if the teacher wishes to break this subject in a sensitive manner and to problematize the topic at hand beyond language acquisition in the English classroom, the short movie *Dumb Ways to Die* can be considered as highly useful.

1 Where to Find the Shorty and the Legal Implications of its Use

Melbourne Metropolitan Transport has developed the video entitled *Dumb Ways to Die* as an educational video to inform commuters about possible dangers as often encountered within underground and / or railway stations and to ask them to avoid any risks. The short music clip (the song sung by *Tangerine Kitty* being the bone and marrow of the video) is highly entertaining and its text and the visuals that come along show cute little jellybeans who (which?[2]) end their lives in a rather unfortunate (if not to say »dumb«) manner. Why? In a nutshell: to draw attention to serious railway accidents and how the former can be

---

[1] If you are in need of further information, the Wikipedia entry is highly revealing and illuminating alike: https://en.wikipedia.org/wiki/Darwin_Awards (as retrieved on Oct 2nd 2016)

[2] The little characters appear rather human despite their amorphous features. Henceforth they will be treated as persons.

prevented. Before the content will be laid out in a more detailed manner, a few legal recommendations as to the use of this clip in a classroom context should be mentioned.

Since the song, just as much as the animations, is copyrighted, it would be much better *to stream* the video live in the computer lab than *to download* it in any – possibly highly illegal – manner. Thus, the lesson and approaches suggested in this article would best be implemented in a computer lab as most schools dispose of these days anyway. The quality of the stream is good enough to make any of the upcoming suggestions work.

You can look for the title *Dumb Ways to Die* on any common search engine such as *Google, Yahoo* or *Qwant* and the first hit usually represents the video used here. Or you just go directly to common clip and video services such as *Vimeo, Youtube* or *Clipfish* and type in the former name. Some of the respective web pages would comprise these:

https://www.youtube.com/watch?v=IJNR2EpS0jw
https://vimeo.com/53831314 (all URLs as retrieved on October 3rd 2016).

Whether you run the clip up front or have the pupils retrieve it on their computers should be within the scope of your didactic choices. Just let it be noted once more that it should by all means be *streamed*. Lastly, make sure you use the original, since there have been numerous spin-offs who took advantage of the fact that the clip viewed here became so popular that even a computer-game was developed alongside. The clip grew into a viral hit on the web a few years ago – the ads for these apps comprise the same jellybean characters, who, of course, also leave for the netherworld in a rather unpleasant yet highly entertaining manner.

2 The Content of the Clip Explained

Dying, of course, is anything else but assuredly not a laughing matter. Or is it? Seen the way it is presented within this *shorty*, it becomes one at least. A group of featureless, yet somehow humanoid jellybeans finish themselves off whilst smiling and accepting their fate gracefully and line-dancing as corpses later on.

Their dumb mistakes are documented within the stanzas of the song that is sung along and really is inviting kids to tune in – or even better: to sing along. The chorus serves as a sort of a reminder of all the fatal pranks as the jellybean corpses perform their little ballet, where evidence of their passing away is clearly visible. The first two stanzas as seen below and the chorus in between address this very bluntly, though in quite a funny manner – even more so as soon as you take into account the animations and the music by *Tangerine Kitty*, the artist performing the song, which remotely reminds listeners of a country-song or a nursery rhyme. The lyric sample chosen to illustrate the principle runs like this:

Set fire to your hair
Poke a stick at a grizzly bear
Eat medicine that's out of date
Use your private parts as piranha bait

Dumb ways to die
so many dumb ways to die
Dumb ways to die-ie-ie
so many dumb ways to die

Get your toast out with a fork
Do your own electrical work
Teach yourself how to fly
Eat a two week old unrefridgerated pie [...][3]

It should be obvious why this could be considered an entertaining and motivating way of conducting an English lesson – be it focused on grammar, on vocabulary or an ethical view of the subject of *death:* the dangers are presented in a sarcastic and yet abstract manner, all of which even becomes a bit more light-hearted when listening to the »soundtrack« by *Tangerine Kitty*.

3 Why This Particular Short Clip? Didactic Reflections Beforehand

Serious deliberations taking into account a class's situation should precede any use of this video – the motivational value of the clip at hand should by no means outweigh other factors that a teacher undeniably needs to consider. Showing a video such as this to teenagers always needs to be pondered on for one and very specific reason: Some of the pupils might already have grown sensitive to the issue of *death*, for example because some of their relatives passed away early or because they are experiencing psychological troubles (phenomena as depression or suicidal thoughts not being uncommon with nowadays' teenagers). Thus, educators have to weigh the pros and cons of using the video very carefully, taking into account the various dispositions of their addressees. If in doubt, the learning sequences as suggested within this article should rather be skipped for empathy's or compassion's sake.

---

3   own tapescript

However, if – or when – all of these former doubts can be set aside, the clip *Dumb Ways to Die* appears to be a real treasure grove for English lessons – for various reasons.

First of all, the relatively short length of the video allows one to come up with lesson structures that can be rounded off within one school period of 45 to 60 minutes, thus avoiding any conflict with time[4]. Another criterion for the choice of this particular *shorty* is the linguistic level used. While some of the items of vocabulary are exotic to learners of late secondary stage 1 or early secondary stage 2, others are already well-known to them. On top of that, the visualisation chosen helps to illustrate the unknown vocabulary as clearly as only possible. Should any problem of comprehension arise, the clip can be replayed several times (although not too many, otherwise its initial »fun-factor« for learners would fade). Nearly last, but not at all least, the idea to use video-clips complies very much with German – and in particular – Bavarian syllabi, which stipulate quite explicitly that *audio-visual* comprehension needs to be integrated within any language acquisition process.[5]

Finally, the fact that the video *Dumb Ways to Die* need not be bought or borrowed is also a factor not to be neglected. *Streaming* a video in the computer lab or – even better – having groups of pupils stream it to differentiate among learners' paces or tasks is one last and yet significant argument for its didactic use.

4 Ideas for Classroom Use

Some of the upcoming suggestions are pretty straightforward and, undoubtedly, »it has all been said before« – thus the article's author does not take any credit for quite common ideas of classroom interaction. Still, these suggestions are meant as hints and inspiration for teachers of English, leaving room for further didactic ideas of their own.

---

[4] see Thaler, Engelbert (2012): Englisch unterrichten. Berlin: Cornelsen. 68. Several criteria for picking a suitable audio-visual format are explained in a very concise manner here. Another more comprehensive list of criteria, especially for short movie formats, is available in the following publication: Thaler, Engelbert (2014): Teaching English with Films. Parderborn: Schöningh, 78 ff.

[5] For further information, see for example the *Fachprofil Englisch* of Bavarian grammar schools as to be seen on http://www.isb-gym8-lehrplan.de (October 6th 2016); or check the respective syllabi for each age tier on the same webpage, where audio-visual »texts« are mentioned repeatedly as an authentic source to be used to instigate learning processes and to foster the development of communicative competence.

4.1 If-clauses in Practice

The video shows one thing quite clearly: the fact that outright stupid behaviour such as keeping rattlesnakes as pets has *consequences*. Nothing is more straightforward hence than to mould this logic link between reason and consequence into its linguistic form: *if-clauses*. Ideally, pupils already have acquired the grammatical structures of if-clauses type I, type II and type III to verbalise and to describe the content of the clip. If the rules are already known, the video just serves as a prompt for exercise.

For instance, learners can be asked to answer questions as asked by the teacher whilst freeze-framing the video at the little round-up dance of »corpses« (here, if-clauses type III are at stake):

> *Teacher: »If **jellybean 1 had not taught** itself how to fly but had asked some instructor, what **would have happened**?«*
> *Pupil (ideally): »The **jellybean would not have crashed** and **would have founded** a family of cute little jellybeans.«*
> *Teacher: »And if **his friend had not done** his own electrical work?«*
> *Pupil (ideally): »The **jellybean would not have been hit** by lightning or **been electrocuted**« ...*[6]

This could evolve into a tandem exercise or several students could be called to the front in order to point out their »favourite corpse« while asking questions in the teacher's place.

Alternatively, the video can be used to introduce if-clauses inductively by showing several parts of the video. The respective parts of the student-teacher-interaction should then be visualised up front to make pupils discover the rule on their own (either take down the relevant structures while talking or prepare a transparency / computer slide beforehand). Here, type II of if-clauses could easily be elicited by stopping the clip at the relevant time indexes:

> *Teacher: »If **you / I / somebody used** my private parts as piranha bait, what **would happen**?«*
> *Pupil (ideally): »**You** probably **would be bitten**.«*
> *Teacher : »And if **I poked** a stick at a grizzly bear?«*
> *Pupil (ideally): »**The bear would eat** you alive.«*
> *Teacher: »OK, let's start the video again and see whether you are right.«*

Thus, a neat structure would develop on the blackboard or on the projector, which would allow learners to come up with the relevant grammatical rule of

---

6   All teacher-pupil dialogues, of course, are just idealised versions of possible classroom discourse meant to illustrate possible forms of prompting, elicitation and progression.

conditional I vs. *simple past* quite easily; and all of this while using some gripping examples that stick to their memories for a long time (remember: their teacher might be bitten by piranhas or be eaten alive!). A chain or group exercise could be used here, too – the pupil just having answered is asked to come up with the next question shortly after he was shown the relevant seconds of the clip. He / she will then call up some pupil to answer who will then have to find the subsequent question and so on.

The very same procedure could also be used when talking about if-clauses type I, stopping the clip over and over again to show the link between cause and consequence (*Teacher: »What will happen if I set fire to my hair? Well, let's see. ... Ah, my head will burn.«*).

In summary, whether you use the several structures inductively or deductively, the video allows teachers to introduce all three types of if-clauses just as much as to have pupils revise and practice the various rules that come along – and the examples might all be a bit more entertaining than anything the pupils find in the textbooks.

4.2 Making Predictions: Expressions of Futurity

It goes without saying that if-clauses and the expression of consequences is closely linked to the expression of *future* events. Although native speakers of many parts of *anglophonia* do not really consciously differentiate between rules for some of the several ways to describe future events, many learners who learn English as a second language are asked to comply with certain rules in this respect (e.g. simple present as the so-called *time-table future* and for axiomatic truths, *going-to-future* based on present evidence, *will-future* as a neutral way to predict events, ...). *Dumb Ways to Die* allows one to apply these rules by rote. Many a sentence on the content of the video can be formed using one of these expressions of futurity. Quite coincidently, learners will also come to understand that the use of one of these expressions often depends very much *on the perspective* the speaker has on the events he or she is aiming to describe. For example, is being eaten by a bear (after you have poked him) an axiomatic truth / consequence (*simple present* hence), a neutral prediction by a bystander (*will-future*) or part of your immediate personal future based on present evidence (*going-to-future*)?

And yet again, the clip could just be seen as a prompt for oral or written exercise of these expressions or it could be used to introduce some of the rules. Once again a technique of freezing the video seems to be an appropriate choice (for example when the hair that has been set alight is ablaze or when the fork is being shoved into the toaster) – only then the teacher can elicit the future outcome of this stupid behaviour whilst asking for the exact grammatical phenomenon (e.g. *going-to-future*). As seen in 4.1, it might also be fun for the learners to freeze the video when the little corpses dance along with the chorus. However, here the learners should not have seen the previous stanza (where the fatality is explained in words and pictures). Then the teacher could enquire in the following manner (take into account screenshot 3 above):

> Teacher: »When **will you be stuck** in a tumble-dryer?«
> Pupil (ideally): »When I choose it as a hiding place.«
> Teacher: »And when **will somebody lose** his lower flesh whilst keeping his torso?«
> Pupil (ideally): »Maybe when you go swimming with piranhas or sharks.«

In the end, quite a few manners of practicing and / or introducing grammatical rules can be put into action with this *freeze-frame* technique.

4.3 Witnessing the Present Consequences of Past Events

The last grammatical phenomenon that can be practiced or developed in just the same manner is the *present perfect*, a tense which always confronts German (and also other) learners with some difficulties, since the logical concept of a past tense that bears a close relation to the present is utterly unknown in their mother tongue.

As far as the clip discussed here is concerned, nowhere does this become more obvious than within the little corpses' dance; the jellybean *having died* of the consumption of a »two week old unrefridgerated pie« still has vomit on his face and his friend who *has messed* with a bear is only present in half as the bear *has bitten* off his upper body. Thus the tense could once more be explained or practiced. For instance, pupils can be asked when they look at the freeze-frame of the dance:

> Teacher (pointing at one of the »corpses«): »Now how **has** this character **died**?«
> Pupil 1 (ideally): »He **has messed** with a bear.«

Once again this could be organised as a chain exercise, where the pupil who has delivered the right answer is called up front and is supposed to ask the subsequent question, pointing at another of the »victims«; thus a pupil-centred speaking activity would develop, in which the teacher will only intervene if linguistic trouble or disturbances arise:

> Pupil 1 (who just gave the right answer): »Now how **has** this character **died**?«
> Pupil 2 (ideally): »He **has done** his own electrical work. How **has** this character **left** the world?«
> Pupil 3 (ideally): »He **has taught** himself how to fly. And what about this one, how **has** he **passed** away?« [...]

Especially grammatical phenomena that are hard to grasp for learners should not only be presented by activating cognitive channels, but also be »engraved« in the learners' memory by pattern exercise – in this case the topic and sarcasm of the video will enhance this memory effect as it also opens up an emotional channel: black humour.

All three uses explained above (4.1 through 4.3) will demand that the video is stopped, restarted, maybe rewound or replayed in bits – this, of course, is in itself demotivating and will take away a bit of the fun. One solution to grapple with this might be to promise the learners to watch one of the spin-offs (using a second video of the same name) as an incentive if they do well, thus maintaining motivation at its initial level when the video was played completely as an attention grabber at the start of the lesson for example.

Moreover, the uses explained afore are up to the teacher's choice – in any case the video will allow to develop and elicit new forms, it will allow to practice them just as much as it will help to differentiate certain grammatical phenomena.

4.4 *To Set Your Head Ablaze with Knowledge*: Vocabulary

Having seen the very innovative and sometimes really cruel ways of dying the heroes of the clip invent, it seems very straightforward to also have pupils work on the vocabulary that is concerned with all matters of death.

Considering the fact that nearly two scores of characters find their way into the netherworld, also pupils will come to understand that finding synonyms for this action should be handy in the description of the video. This would also allow to differentiate a bit further between certain registers, the colloquial one assuredly being more appropriate to the video. Some of the expressions will hence be just as much tongue-in-cheek as the whole tone of the clip. Pupils could work in tandems using a dictionary, but also classic teacher input could easily breach the subject – as a result, a list with items such as *to pass on, to decease, to die, to exhale one's last breath, to depart this life, to perish, to meet your maker, to kick the bucket, to go six feet under, to have reached one's expiry date* will be developing.

Yet another idea might be to elaborate word fields surrounding one manner in which the jellybeans perish; e.g. one of them sets fire to its hair, so useful items of vocab would of course include *to set alight, to be ablaze, to burn down, to suffer burns, to smoulder, to crackle, to be a living torch* and so on.

The same holds true for the different kinds of animals that the poor victims encounter for the last time, a list which could easily be extended relying on the pupils' background knowledge (surely a motivating task): *to be bitten to death by a tiger, to be hunted down by a lion, to be chased up a tree by a bear, to be eaten alive by piranhas, to be poisoned by a snake's venom, to be stung by a scorpion, to be trampled to death by an elephant, to be dragged down by a shark etc.* Organising this as a mere list is probably too demotivating, activation of pupils would hence imply to make them draw up illustrated charts (possibly with the pictures of the animals involved) or to have them design mind-maps (with the usual risk of getting an unorganised result for the latter form).

Especially the scenes of line-dancing will also illustrate the vocabulary for the manners in which the little heroes die: one is *tumble-dried to death*, the next one *dies of food poisoning* (of having eaten an unrefridgerated pie), one *crashed with his plane*, somebody else *died of drug intoxication* (the medicine was out of date).

No matter which approach the teacher uses, the realm of words needed to describe the video in its full richness of detail is nearly infinite. Methodical choices to activate pupils should of course coincide with the use of this video – freeze-framing the video, equipping students with a decent dictionary (the use of which could also be trained here) and asking them to keep a record of the results found worthy of showing to their classmates are thus paramount; otherwise the motivational surplus as created by the fun approach to the subject will quickly trickle off (nothing is more boring than establishing or copying a simple list of words!). Preferably, some further visualisation of the items at stake is also left to the pupils (animals could be imprinted, different noises made by fire could be illustrated by drawings, ...). Like this, learners will be kept avid of extending their range of vocabulary.

5 Dying – Not a Laughing Matter: Reflections Beyond Language

The *pre-, while-* and *post-viewing* models of teaching movies and clips have been around for a while. All the language applications as explained in the preceding chapter were mostly relying on activities which were to take place *while* viewing, some of the tasks also »priming« pupils' language output in a sense of expressing *pre-viewing* premonitions and ideas of what is about to come.

In view of the ethically relative complex issue at stake, i.e. *dying* (which, in the course of this particular clip, is ridiculed and played down as the ultimate pun in the life of those little jellybeans), *post-viewing* activities should be considered to be compulsory.

Especially the »Rezeptionsgespräch« (or in English roughly: discussion of receptive impressions)[7] must by no means be left out. Students have to be given

---

7 see, for example, Surkamp, Carola (2004): Teaching Films: Von der Filmanalyse zu handlungs- und prozessorientierten Formen der filmischen Textarbeit. In: Der fremdsprachliche Unterricht Englisch 68, 7.

the chance to also articulate their personal concerns, their personal experience and their individual feelings about the subject of *dying*. In this respect the use of the video can reach beyond the acquisition of language, as it can integrate the children into the lesson or course in a very empathic and also emotional manner – and all of this with a topic that sometimes is easily set aside or even a taboo in a vivid setting full of adolescents such as school. Some of the guiding questions to be asked by the teacher that will allow a deeper reflection of the topic of *death* might include the following:

- *What is your personal experience with death? Have you already lost some relative?*
- *Why is sarcasm and humour a humane way of grappling with this cruel topic?*
- *Why is it a topic that we should discuss here at school / in English class as well?*
- *Why do we laugh at cartoonlike characters suffering severe accidents when the latter would be highly tragic in real everyday life?*
- *Why is it that dying is very often ridiculed or played down?*
- *etc.*

Especially in higher grades, a vivid discussion will hopefully evolve, allowing pupils to reflect the very express *absence* of death in everyday conversation and occupations (although the act of *passing on* is, of course, in store for every individual at some future point of time) and the relative *omnipresence* of *death* in the media and its voyeuristic exploitation by such phenomena as the *Darwin Award* or in TV and cinematic productions (death being an element of dramaturgy).

Consequently, this discussion and ethical approach would channel into media criticism that will also allow to reflect the use and intentions of the clip *Dumb Ways to Die*. Once more here are a few suggestions of what might be examined:

- *Why would Melbourne Metropolitan Trains have somebody produce such a video?*
- *Why did they use cartoons of jellybeans and not stuntmen?*
- *Why is the underlying soundtrack happy and catchy?*
- *Where and how would you distribute the clip?*
- *Who is the target group at which the clip is aiming?*
- *Should its viewing be restricted in terms of age?*
- *Could there be another purpose behind the clip?*
- *etc.*

Ultimately, this kind of reflection would possibly also lead to productive steps as the last logic link to conclude the unit based on this shorty. Having thought through the nature of the topic just as much as the mediatized use of the clip, a few *post-viewing* activities could make pupils rethink the video in its content as well as in its linguistic outlay: they could be asked to write another storyboard, to find alternate endings for each of the victims' lives, they could come up with (and maybe even produce) another soundtrack to the clip, they might find different uses for the poor jellybeans (e.g. could there be a video advertising for a smoking ban?). Students might also be asked whether they could review or criticise the clip for their local newspaper, whether they could enact some of the scenes as a short play (careful with the props though) or whether they could develop a *sequel* or a *prequel* and so on. The amount of productive tasks based on a *post-viewing* reflection of *Dumb Ways To Die* is next to infinite – however, a first critical contemplation with some guidance by the teacher must by no means be skipped (see questions above). Otherwise the productive output might and will at times develop in unwanted directions.

All in all, especially in higher grades, the shorty *Dumb Ways to Die* will also allow to probe and to improve the pupils' grasp of complex moral issues just as much as to challenge them to question the purposes and functioning of this kind of medium and similar forms of advertisement.

6 All Things Said and Done – One Shorty and a Range of Didactic Choices

Having explored all the uses and possible activities to be conducted and instigated within a classroom full of learners of English, the clip *Dumb Ways To Die* should, of course, not be treated as an isolated example. Be it the linguistic aspects of the video or the ethical discussion ensuing, the video should by all means be integrated in a steady and long-term process of education and language teaching. In the case of *if-clauses* this might only engulf a short period of several lessons where the learning success will easily be operationable in terms of assessment; in the case of media criticism and discussion of values, the outcome has to be considered in the long run, also taking into account and accepting indeterminacies, personal attitudes and the perspectives that other subjects (such as other foreign languages) offer to the pupils.

In conclusion, *Dumb Ways to Die* will provide learners with a much saner, much more reflected stance towards the topic of *death* if presented in the right manner – and this while delivering a motivational surplus to the English classroom just as much as many a possibility to pick up structures and vocabulary.

Bibliography

Print

Surkamp, Carola (2004): *Teaching Films:* Von der Filmanalyse zu handlungs- und prozessorientierten Formen der filmischen Textarbeit. In: Der fremdsprachliche Unterricht Englisch 68. 2-12.

Thaler, Engelbert (2012): Englisch unterrichten. Berlin: Cornelsen.

Thaler, Engelbert (2014): Teaching English with Films. Parderborn: Schöningh.

Online

N.N. *Bavarian Syllabus for Grammar Schools.* http://www.isb-gym8-lehrplan.de (Stand: 06.10.2016)

N.N. *Darwin Awards Background Info.* https://en.wikipedia.org/wiki/Darwin_Awards (Stand: 02.10.2016)

N.N. *Dumb Ways to Die (clip).* https://www.youtube.com/watch?v=IJNR2EpS0jw (Stand: 03.10.2016)

N.N. *Dumb Ways to Die (clip).* https://vimeo.com/53831314 (Stand: 03.10.2016)

»Father and Daughter« - An Animation Film for All Foreign Languages

Genia Markova, Jana Pessozki

The reflection of the father's role while dealing with the loss of a parent is a difficult issue that affects many young people today. This topic is central to the silent short film »Father and Daughter«, which, despite the absence of dialogues, has a great potential for analysis and interpretation.

The topic of »family life and parent-child relationship« occupies a central place in foreign language teaching worldwide. The short silent animation film »Father and Daughter« (Michaël Dudok de Wit, 2000) tells a very special story of a loss. Artful and elaborate, using only music and pictures to convey the message, the film is suitable for use in all foreign language courses and at different levels of the Common European Framework of Reference for Languages (CEFR). Within the framework of the teaching unit presented here, the following skills are promoted: visual comprehension, writing and film analysis. Besides that, students will expand their vocabulary related to the topics of »emotions« and »family«.

1 The Film

The short film »Father and Daughter«, produced in 2000, received over 20 international awards; among other honors, it was named the best animation short film at the 2001 Oscars. The film tells a sad story of a girl who was abandoned by her father and who suffers from this loss for the rest of her life. It remains open whether he simply goes away or dies. Sketchy and simple, but very touching, the film offers a good opportunity to deal with the motifs of »love«, »loss« and »loneliness«. Missing dialogues or monologues motivate students to put the story into their own words at language levels B1, B2 and C1 of the CEFR. Due to its sensitive subject matter, emphasis is put on writing instead of speaking. The manageable film length (about 9 minutes) allows a detailed analysis and interpretation within a maximum of three double period classes. Thanks to its subject matter and multimediality, the film is suitable for cross-curricular learning: the fields of ethics, music and art can support foreign language teaching harmoniously.

2 The Teaching Unit

2.1 Pre-viewing activities

On the basis of some screenshots, the students should first express their expectations of the film. Weaker learners can receive a vocabulary aid to express feelings (worksheet 1). An alternative would be to simply play the film's music track and then to ask the students to express their expectations. One can find the film on youtube.

2.2 While-viewing activities

After the first viewing, comprehension is tested (worksheet 2). Exercises 2 and 3 are designed for weaker courses; advanced students can concentrate on the tasks 1 and 4.

2.3 Post-viewing activities

2.3.1 Writing a summary

Students practise writing a summary in this step of the lesson unit (worksheet 3). Task 1 prepares them for criteria-oriented writing. Those students who need more support can work at task 1 b), in which they search for errors in the given summary. They also have to restructure the text and fill in the necessary linking words.

2.3.2 Analysis and interpretation of cinematic devices

The complex task of film analysis and interpretation is designed as a jigsaw puzzle activity (task 2). This method is suitable for cooperation and differentiation according to levels of difficulty. Five groups of students focus on music, colours, symbols, structural elements, camera position and camera perspective.

The groups working with film music can receive a list of vocabulary with the names of musical instruments or use a dictionary. The group which analyses film symbols may use the Internet for specific research of symbols used in the film. Another possibility is to give them a list of options with several wrong ones, which they can match to the symbols. Should film analysis be difficult for your students, this aspect of analysis can be omitted.

The grid will help your students to acquire knowledge of different aspects of analysis and interpretation of cinematic devices. They should learn that in the first step one describes what is seen or heard in the scene, and then interprets it referring to the context and giving reasons. Finally, students should discern which cinematic devices play a more important role in this film, how all of them harmonize and what their effects on the viewers are.

2.3.3 Creative writing

Task 3, which aims at the development of creative writing skill, allows students to choose individually which of the possible text formats they prefer to work at. Alternatively the group can decide together which writing task(s) they would like to choose. The range of text formats varies from a personal letter, interior monologue, film review, diary entry, mini-saga to a shape poem. These types of texts correspond well with the film because students will write from the protagonists' perspectives and thus feel empathy for them. Film symbols can be of use in writing a shape poem (e.g., a wheel, a tree or a boat). Moreover, students have a possibility to use their artistic talents.

After the texts are written, students should give each other feedback in a writing conference. For this purpose they need feedback sheets with evaluation criteria (which they should be made aware of before they start writing). This method makes transparent evaluation possible and as a consequence helps to improve the texts effectively. After the texts are improved, they are presented to the whole group and are acknowledged. If students wish so, they can publish a portfolio with their texts or present them on the school website.

3 Conclusion

Due to their countless advantages, silent films have been used in foreign language teaching for a long time. The animation film »Father and Daughter« is an original and aesthetically valuable material to use in a lesson unit on the topic of »parent-child relationships« or »great losses«. It will definitely appeal to young viewers. The differentiated and creative task formats as well as cooperative patterns of interaction in the teaching unit presented above will develop your students' writing skills and their film analysis competences.

Worksheet 1

Pre-viewing task

- We are going to watch a short animated film called »Father and Daughter« (it is about 9 minutes long). It won an Oscar award in 2001 and many other film awards. Look at the snapshots from the film.
- What do you expect to see? What kind of storyline could the film have? What kind of relationship between the father and his daughter could it show?
- Fill in the grid with nouns, adjectives and verbs, which describe different feelings. They might help you to express your expectations.

Emotions	Nouns	Adjectives	Verbs
Love			
Joy			
Hatred			
Sadness			

Worksheet 2

While-viewing task
- Which of the predictions you expressed before watching were close to the film?
- Mark if the statements in the grid below are true or false. Correct the false ones.

	True	False
a) The father leaves his daughter when she is just a teenager.		
b) The daughter keeps coming back to the place where she saw her father for the last time.		
c) The girl has to row a boat each time she wants to reach this special place.		
d) The girl's life is ruined and she is not able to start a family of her own.		
e) The film shows the important role of parents in our lives even if they are absent.		

- Build an opinion line in the classroom: those of you who would give the film 10 points should stand near the blackboard. Those who would give the film 5 points stay in the middle of the classroom, the back of the room will mean 0 points for the film. Any number like 3 or 7 should be somewhere in between. Be ready to explain your decisions.

Worksheet 3

Post-viewing tasks

1. Writing a summary

Watch the film for the second time and choose task a) OR b)

a) Take notes on the aspects in the grid below. Compare your notes with those of your partner.
   Then write a well-structured summary. Use linking words. Remember that you should only write what you see and not what you think or feel. Don't interpret! Use the simple present tense.

Here are some facts you will need for the introduction:
Director and author of the script: Michaël Dudok de Wit
Release dates: 2000, UK / Belgium / Netherlands

Protagonists (main and minor)	
Setting	Where:
	When:
What happens (the plot)	– father and daughter ride bikes
	– they come to …

b) Read the summary of the film. Find mistakes or aspects that should not be in a summary. Rewrite it without unnecessary information. Divide the text into paragraphs and use linking words (suddenly, finally, later, etc.).

A father says goodbye to his young daughter and leaves on a boat. As the wide landscapes live through their seasons, so the girl lived through hers. Birds are flying in the sky and the trees are very beautiful. The girl keeps coming to the place where she parted with her father. Near this place there is a wide and fast river. She is always on a bike. She becomes a young woman with a beautiful face, has a family of her own and in time she becomes old, yet within her there is always a deep longing for her father. At the end of the film, in what appears to be a dream sequence, or perhaps the afterlife, they are reunited. I think she died and met her father again. The atmosphere of the film is very sad and the music supports this feeling. There are many visual symbols, which create a sad atmosphere.

2. *Film analysis*

a. Make groups and describe the aspect you are responsible for. Decide together on the functions and effects of your aspect.
b. Make mixed groups of experts and exchange the results of your work. Decide which of the examined devices make a bigger impact on you as viewers (At which point did you feel especially strong emotions?).

Use these verbs to talk about functions/aspects: to symbolize, to stand for, to mean, to contrast, to support/ to match, to emphasize, to create a/an ... atmosphere, to support ... mood, to remind of, to resemble, to represent, to evoke the feeling of ..., to underline ...

Cinematic aspects	Descriptions	Effects/ functions
Group 1: Music – Describe the music in the film. Find adjectives for the music in different sequences of the film. – Which musical instruments play in the foreground in different film sequences? How do they sound? – Does music match or contrast with the images?		

Cinematic aspects	Descriptions	Effects/ functions
Group 2: Symbols and metaphors What do these objects stand for in the film? - Boat - Water (river or lake) - Wheel/ Road - Tree - Bird - Hill - Wind		
Group 3: Colours What colours do the filmmakers use in the film? Do they match or contrast with the images?		
Group 4: Structural aspects - Find the key moments in the film. - What kind of women does the main protagonist meet on her way to the hill? Compare them with her and explain the effect. - Examine how the main protagonists appear in these scenes. - Find some examples of repetition and accumulation (enumeration) in the film. Explain their effect. - What happens to the main protagonist in the last scene?		
Group 5: Field sizes and camera positions - Examine the types of shots in the film and why they are used in different sequences (extreme close-up, close-up, medium shot, full shot and long shot, extreme long shot). - Which camera positions and angles are mostly used (establishing shot, bird's eye view/high-angle shot, frog's perspective/low-angle shot, eye-level shot)? - Why don't we see close-ups and extreme close-ups in the film?		

3. Creative writing tasks (choose the one you like!)

> **STEP 1:** Make the first draft. Let a partner, who writes the same task (or teacher), check it (use criteria grids for feedback). Rewrite the text, improving it.
> **STEP 2:** Make a silent »all-you-can read« activity, in which you read as many texts of your classmates as you can without commenting at first. Then decide which of the texts were very good. Explain your opinion in a plenary.
> **STEP 3:** Make a digital portfolio of the whole group with different texts based on the film. Why not publish it on your school website?

- Imagine that you are the girl. Today you went to the hill again and thought about your father. Write a diary entry about this day. Describe your feelings, fears and dreams.
- Imagine that you are the father. Write a letter to your daughter explaining what happened from your perspective.
- Imagine that you are the girl's friend. You know how much she misses her dad. Write a letter to her giving advice on how to cope with her problem.
- Write a film review for a school magazine.
- Write an interior monologue of the girl/woman in form of a »voice-over« for the film.
- Write a mini-saga based on the film. A mini-saga is a text which sums up the content like a summary, it can still be creative and must have no more than fifty words including the title.
- Write a shape poem from the girl's perspective. Take one of the symbolic objects from task 2 for your poem, e.g. a boat, a tree, a bird, a river or a wheel. Draw it. Write your text in the picture/ in the object. You don't need rhymes in a shape poem. Its structure and the way your text harmonises with the picture will make it special.

Here is an example of a shape poem:

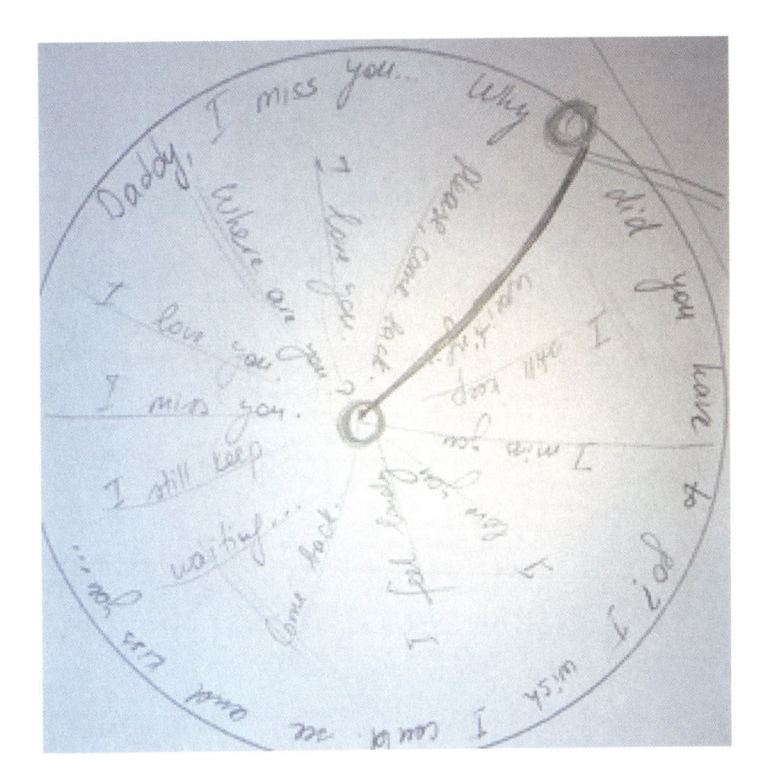

Fig. 1: Shape poem

Bibliography

Link to the film: www.youtube.com/watch?v=miGQrV7uE08 (12.07.2016). Green Line Oberstufe (2015). Stuttgart/ Leipzig: Ernst Klett Verlag, S. 285.
Sicher ins Zentralabitur. Arbeitsheft mit CD-Rom (2006). Stuttgart: Ernst Klett Verlag, S. 82.
Green Line Oberstufe (2015). Stuttgart/Leipzig: Ernst Klett Verlag, S. 290
Green Line Oberstufe (2015). Stuttgart/Leipzig: Ernst Klett Verlag, S. 285
Thaler, Engelbert (2009). Method Guide. Kreative Methoden für den Literaturunterricht in den Klassen 7–12. Paderborn: Schöningh.

C. Lessons

New Silent Short Films

Lena Heinze

1 Genre

The first person to »create the illusion of motion« with photographs was Muybridge in 1877 (Klepper 1999: 5). From then on, all films were naturally silent, as the soundtrack had not been invented yet. Nevertheless, the showings were not only a visual experience for the spectators as a live orchestra or pianist usually provided background music. Sometimes there were even live narrators, who recited the dialogues of the film. This period is often called »classic silent era« and goes on until 1927. In that year, *The Jazz Singer* was the first film with synchronized sound. As to the length of the films, they were not two hours long at the beginning of film history, but rather short for technical reasons.

Nowadays there is a revival of short films and some of them are created as silent short films, which is why this contemporary phenomenon is called »new silent shorts«. Donaghy (2015: 275 ff.) recognizes great teaching value for the TEFL classroom:

- As many short films are artistic, they have limited appeal in the commercial marketplace, so to make them easier to sell all around the globe, they often contain little or no dialogue, which makes comprehension easier.
- They offer intensely cinematic experiences, using images and movement, sequence and duration, sound and music.
- They are great for the language classroom as they can be used with any level – the teacher just needs to adapt the difficulty of the task to match the level of the students.
- Students have to compensate for the lack of dialogues by creating their own spoken or written output.

The short film *Gift*, which the following lesson plans are based on, can be categorized under several genres of short film: social shorts, branded shorts, viral shorts, but this teaching approach will use it from the perspective of new silent short films. »*Gift*« by Zsófia Zsemberi (2015) can be adapted for learners at different levels – in this case A1+ and B1+. This film was also chosen because the topic of pet adoption and abandonment is highly relevant for students as many teenagers have or would like to have a pet, which makes them sensitive to the issue of animal abandonment.

2 Procedure

Lesson A (LOWER GRADES)

Title	Gift (4:36 minutes) (https://www.youtube.com/watch?v=JMs7dkdO4YY)
Synopsis	A family adopts a little girl for their daughter's birthday. They play with her at first but after some time they lose their interest in the girl. Consequently, the girl seeks the family's attention, and since she does not get any, messes up a room. This leads to a fight and the father takes the girl to abandon her in the wilderness. When he drives away, we see that the girl was actually a dog. The last shot shows the caption »Be responsible. Give, adopt wisely.«
Competences	Listening-viewing, speaking, writing, lexical competence
Topics	Gifts, pets, family, relationships, feelings
Level	Lower intermediate
Time	45 min.
Steps (Global-to-detail-approach) A. Lead-in 1. Realia: T shows S a wrapped gift and has S describe it. 2. T asks S about the best gift they have ever received. 3. T tells S they are going to watch a film called *Gift* and has S predict what the film may be about. B. First viewing The video is played straight through. C. Global comprehension 1. »What is the gift?« 2. »Did the ending surprise you? Why (not)?« 3. »What does the insert at the end of the film say? (*Be responsible. Give, adopt wisely.*) 4. »What does that mean?« D. Second viewing The video is shown again.	

E. Detailed understanding
1. S put the film scenes into the right order, and write sentences to revise the plot (M 1).
2. S carry out a word search about adjectives (M 2).
3. S match adjectives with characters and situations of the film, and discuss their answers with a partner (M 3).

F. Follow-up (Homework)
S are asked to write the story from the dog's perspective. They should use adjectives to describe the dog's feelings and help the reader imagine their story better. They can choose between two variations:
1. Retell the plot with the help of the pictures from the previous task.
2. Continue the story.

Lesson B (HIGHER GRADES)

Title	Gift (see above)
Synopsis	See above
Competences	Listening-viewing, media competence, writing, speaking, reading
Topics	adopting / abandoning a pet, responsibility, humanization of animals
Level	Upper-intermediate to advanced
Time	90 minutes

Steps (pre – while – post)
A. Pre-viewing
1. T asks S what »responsibility« means to them.
2. T tells S they are going to watch a short film called *Gift*, asks them what gift-giving has to do with responsibility, and makes S predict what happens in the film.

B. While-viewing (double viewing)
1. T stops the film at 3:15 min and asks S several questions:
a) What are your impressions of the film so far?
b) What is the gift?
c) What is the relationship between the family and the girl like?
d) What do you think will happen next?
2. S view the film to the end. T asks each S for a spontaneous reaction.
3. The film is presented a second time, and S have to focus on film effects:
a) Are there any situations in the film that hint at the girl's ›real‹ identity?
b) When did you notice a turn in the relationship between the girl and the family?
c) What elements are used in the silent film to help us understand its content?

4. T asks S to refer the final words (*Be responsible. Give, adopt wisely*) to the link between gift-giving and responsibility (see pre-viewing task).
5. Think-pair-share:
»Do you think the message of the film would be stronger with spoken language or if we had known that the girl was a dog from the beginning?«

C. Post-viewing
S get together in pairs and can choose between three tasks (M 1), which they have to present in class later.
1. S reflect on the popularity of the film on YouTube and discuss comments.
2. S collect positive and negative aspects of humanizing animals.
3. S create a checklist for people who want to adopt a pet.

E. Homework
S read a text on pet abandonment, collect reasons and preventive actions, and apply their findings to the story in the film (M 2).

3 Materials

Lesson A (LOWER GRADES)

M1: What a mess!

Watch the film a second time and put these scenes into the right order. Then write one sentence each.

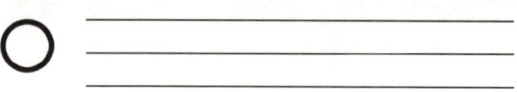

Lessons

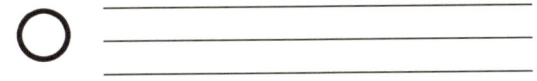

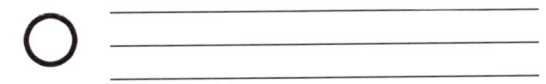

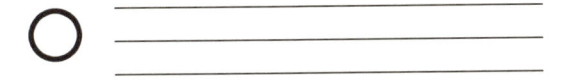

○ _____

○ _____

○ _____

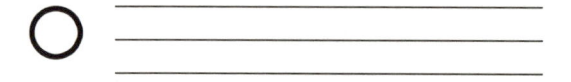

Lena Heinze

Lessons

M 2: Word detective: adjectives

These 12 adjectives are hidden in the puzzle. Can you find them?

happy	surprised	busy
bored	angry	sad
helpless	excited	nice
alone	friendly	annoyed

A	A	V	G	G	O	V	X	V	E	W	F	Z
L	S	N	P	A	L	O	N	E	C	Q	Y	W
S	U	H	N	P	M	F	R	V	V	E	C	M
L	R	E	B	O	S	R	A	C	C	T	H	R
P	P	L	D	A	Y	I	O	I	S	M	R	W
H	R	P	C	G	L	E	N	Z	Q	Y	Y	T
O	I	L	X	N	Q	N	D	I	B	U	S	Y
Z	S	E	K	D	B	D	J	V	D	D	R	T
L	E	S	R	T	D	L	A	Z	P	G	D	J
E	D	S	F	E	Y	Y	P	K	N	A	T	P
R	N	U	R	D	T	H	N	A	S	W	T	B
G	D	O	E	X	C	I	T	E	D	Q	L	Q
C	B	H	A	P	P	Y	W	T	D	I	V	T

M 3: Matching: who, when, why?

Can you match the adjectives with a person and explain the situation?
Work with your partner: One of you completes Part A, the other one Part B.
Look at the example: *The girl is happy because it's her birthday.*

Part A

	Who? (mother, father, girl, dog)	When or why?
happy		
busy		

	Who? (mother, father, girl, dog)	When or why?
excited		
helpless		
angry		
friendly		

Part B

	Who? (mother, father, girl, dog)	When or why?
bored		
surprised		
nice		
annoyed		
alone		
sad		

When you have finished, ask your partner questions to complete the other part. If you do not agree with your partner's answer, discuss.
Example:
B: Who is angry?
A: The girl is angry because she doesn't like dogs.
B: I don't agree with you. I think the mother is angry because the dog has made a mess.

Lesson B (HIGHER GRADES)

M 1: Post-viewing tasks

Gift – a silent short film

In pairs, work on one of the following three topics. Be prepared to present your results later on.

1. YouTube: popularity and comments

a) The film has been watched over 26.7 million times on YouTube. Think of the reasons why people watch and share this video.

b) Take a look at these comments. What are the main claims? Do you agree?

> **CastleFlameGal** 1 month ago
> This is such a good twist. The little girl was really a dog.
> If someone just randomly abandoned a child out like that there would be uproar but if it was a dog, some people would just dismiss it because it's an animal when actually it's exactly the same concept as doing it to a child.
> Reply • 17 👍 👎

> **- Starsong -** 1 week ago
> In my family, we sometimes refer to our pets as 'fur-babies'. To us, they're family. However, I know that there are many people who just don't see it that way. Thank you for this video... I hope it opens people's eyes, and more importantly, their hearts.
> Reply • 2 👍 👎

c) State whether you liked or disliked the film and why.

2. Humanizing animals

a) Why do some people refer to their pets as their children?
b) Do you judge this comparison to be positive or negative?
c) Consider the pictures below: Is there a limit of »humanizing« animals?

Image 1: www.sackstark.info/wp-content/uploads/2008/09/tiergesetz.png
Image 2: www.ratgeberzentralede/fileadmin/_processed_/csm_Hund_nicht_vermenschlichen_52623_Bild2_564f9d4a12.jpg
Image 3: http://static.kleinezeitung.at/images/uploads_520/0/0/d/4083725/pooch726.jpg

3. Pet adoption

a) Imagine you worked at an animal shelter. Set up a checklist for people who consider adopting a pet. You can use ideas from the film or your own experiences.

b) Prepare a dialogue: One of you works at the shelter, your partner is a single working Mum or Dad who wants to give the pet to their kid as a playmate. Use the checklist to decide whether he or she can adopt a pet.

M 2: Homework

Animal Abandonment

Read the text and answer the questions in written form. You may use a dictionary to look up unknown words.

I've been an animal shelter volunteer for more than 10 years. A lot of strays come in the door, but the animals who really touch me are the ones they call the »owner surrenders.« These are the animals who had a home and lost it, and over the years I've tried to understand why people abandon their animal companions. (...)
Sometimes people surrender animals because they think it's the only possible solution. Perhaps someone with a severe cat allergy joins the household, and

the family doesn't realize that these allergies can often be treated or managed. Sometimes people are separated from their animal companions because they become too sick to care for them. Many people don't know about the importance of advance planning for their animal family, and so their animal companions end up in the shelter. Saddest of all is when people die without having made arrangements for their companions. Often these animals are elderly and don't adapt well to the shelter environment. Some of them never make it out of the shelter – they are scared or unfriendly, and potential adopters pass them by. Moving is a frequently given reason for surrender. The paperwork for each animal tells the story: »Moving out of state and cannot take cat.« »New landlord does not allow dogs.« »Found cat in apartment next door after neighbor moved out.« »No space in new home for dog.« But all too often the move is just an excuse. One study showed that more than half of the people surrendering animals because of moving also report behavior problems. In other words, the move often isn't the real issue.

Behavioral problems are the most common reason why people give up their dogs, and they are the second most common reason for cats. Behavioral problems can be very serious, like biting or aggression in dogs. But more often they are common dog and cat issues like inappropriate elimination, destructiveness, barking or meowing, or not getting along with other animals in the home. Sometimes the problem is one of inappropriate expectations: »Cat isn't friendly enough,« or »Dog needs too much attention.« Most behavioral issues can be corrected, but people may lack the knowledge or commitment needed to do the work.

People surrendering an animal with behavior issues don't want to hurt their animal's chances of adoption from the shelter, so they may mislead shelter staff and explain the surrender as due to allergies or a move. This makes it even harder for the shelter to find that animal a suitable home. Or the animal might be adopted, only to be returned by the new guardian as soon as the problem behavior starts.

I've come to believe that one of the most important jobs of an animal shelter is to reduce the number of abandonments through outreach and education. Many animal shelters now have printed information on coping with the most common behavioral problems, and some even provide telephone hotlines to help people work through issues. Shelters can help to educate adopters about the commitment involved in being an animal caregiver. It's also important for anyone thinking about adopting an animal to consider in advance how they will deal with potential issues, so that they don't end up adding to the numbers of abandoned animals.

Source: http://prime.peta.org/2010/01/why-people-abandon-animals

Questions:
a) What are the reasons for abandonment given in the text?
b) What does the writer suggest to prevent abandonment?
c) Think of the film *Gift* again. What was the reason for the family to abandon the dog? Could this have been prevented?

4 Solutions

Lesson A

M 1: Right order of scenes

1. First the man fetches the dog.

2. The girl is happy about her gift.

3. The man doesn't want to play with the dog.

4. The dog has made a mess.

5. The parents are angry with the dog.

6. At the end, the man drives away without the dog.

Lessons

M 2: Word search

A	A	V	G	G	O	V	X	V	E	W	F	Z
L	S	N	P	A	L	O	N	E	C	Q	Y	W
S	U	H	N	P	M	F	R	V	V	E	C	M
L	R	E	B	O	S	R	A	C	C	T	H	R
P	P	L	D	A	Y	I	O	I	S	M	R	W
H	R	P	C	G	L	E	N	Z	Q	Y	Y	T
O	I	L	X	N	Q	N	D	I	B	U	S	Y
Z	S	E	K	D	B	D	J	V	D	D	R	T
L	E	S	R	T	D	L	A	Z	P	G	D	J
E	D	S	F	E	Y	Y	P	K	N	A	T	P
R	N	U	R	D	T	H	N	A	S	W	T	B
G	D	O	E	X	C	I	T	E	D	Q	L	Q
C	B	H	A	P	P	Y	W	T	D	I	V	T

M 3: Matching

	Who? (mother, father, girl, dog)	When or why?
happy	girl	The girl is happy because it is her birthday.
busy	mother	The mother is busy because she is cooking.
excited	girl	The girl is excited when she sees the dog.
helpless	dog	The dog is helpless when the car leaves.
angry	mother	The mother is angry because the dog has made a mess.
friendly	girl	The girl is friendly with the dog at first.
bored	dog	The dog is bored because nobody wants to play with her.
surprised	girl	The girl is surprised because she did not expect to get a dog as a gift.
nice	father	The father is nice to the dog in the car.

	Who? (mother, father, girl, dog)	When or why?
annoyed	father	The father is annoyed with the dog when he works at the computer.
alone	dog	The dog is alone at the end.
sad	dog	The dog is sad because the family does not want her.

F 2: Possible continuation from the dog's perspective:

When the car left, I was really sad. I liked the girl and thought she was my new friend. So I didn't understand why her father didn't take me back home with him. He was so friendly the day he picked me up, but today he didn't look very happy. While I was dreaming of our day at the beach, I heard somebody scream »Barker! No, there's the road! Barker! Come here!«

I was surprised because I thought I was alone on the road. But suddenly there was a dog next to me who touched my nose with his nose. A woman ran behind him and patted me when she saw me. »Oh, now I know why you didn't want to listen. OK, you're right. She is a beautiful dog.« And then they took me with them. I was the happiest dog in the world!

Lesson B

B.3. Film analysis

a. hints at girl's real identity
- Man feeds girl in the car / girl does not touch food with hands (0:41)
- Father and daughter play ball with the girl, the girl walks behind them (daughter and father are holding hands) (1:18)
- Girl is excluded from the table (1:34)
- Girl tugs the mother's blouse (2:15)
- Father tries to lure the girl with her soft-toy to get her out of the house (3:10)

b. turning point
  - At 1:39, the music changes from cheerful to melancholic
  - The scene is dark
  - The emotions towards the girl have changed: Before the family laughed and treated the girl in a friendly way, now they are cold towards her, look angry and desperate

c. techniques to compensate for the lack of dialogues
  - gestures
  - facial expression

- body language
- music
- clear plot
- analogy between child and dog is well portrayed
- caption at the end

C. Post-viewing: Worksheet (M 1)

1. YouTube
a. Popularity:
- the video has a strong / powerful message that is conveyed in a simple way
- it is very emotional, moving
- many people are pet owners and can relate to the topic
- the video raises awareness of abandonment which still happens frequently
- comparison of a child and a pet is well depicted

b. Comments:
- 1st comment: some people care less about animals than children, although pet abandonment is just as bad as child abandonment (according to this user)
- 2nd comment: pets are like babies / children in many families; this video has both a rational and an emotional message

c. Possible attitude:

Wow. This video has changed my mind. I am usually not a big pet lover but the analogy between the child and the dog made me realize the cruelty of abandoning animals. I hope a lot of people will see this and think twice about adopting a pet and the resulting responsibility.

2. Humanizing animals
Positive aspects:
- people who do not have children have a strong bond with their pet, they feel responsible for it and take care of it
- many pet owners want their best for their pet because it is like a family member for them, they provide food and shelter, go to the vet regularly, keep their pets in an appropriate way
- old people with pets have a task, pet gives their life a purpose
- people with handicaps can have companion dogs, there is mutual responsibility between them and their pet

Negative aspects:
- some dogs do not get enough exercise because owners do not want to push them too hard

- some people buy their pets clothes or feed them at the table, which can lead to behavioural problems
- some owners do not feed their pet appropriately, e.g. overfeed them with treats or give them the wrong type of food, which can cause diseases
- there are people who practice docking / cropping / tailing which is against the nature of animals

3. Pet adoption
a. Checklist
  - Why do you want a pet? (commitment, carefully planned idea)
  - What kind of pet suits your lifestyle? (Consider allergies, size of the pet, activities, chores, life expectancy ...)
  - Who is responsible for the pet?
  - Do you have enough time?
  - Do you have enough space, and are you allowed to keep a pet in your house / flat?
  - Can you afford a pet? (food, toys, vet ...)

b. Dialogue (A = shelter employee, B = client)
A: Hi there, how can I help you?

B: Hello. I'm looking for a pet for my daughter. You know, I work a lot so she is quite lonely sometimes. I was thinking of getting her a dog.

A: Ok. Have you ever had a dog or do you have any experience with dogs?

B: No, not yet, but my daughter loves dogs. Whenever we are in the park she plays with them and doesn't want to leave any more.

A: Alright. May I suggest you take a look at our checklist? We require new adopters to go through these questions as we have seen that unfortunately many people don't consider the responsibility that comes with owning a pet.

B: Of course! We do have a nice house with a big garden, we were both tested negative for allergies ...

A: That's good to know and a garden is a great advantage. What about the other points?

B (goes through the checklist): Oh, maybe this could be a problem. I forgot about the fact that the dog would be home alone while my daughter is at school and I'm at work. I'm a single Mum, you see, so it's only the two of us in our household. That's sad. I know she would have taken good care of it.

A: Hmm. I think I can suggest you something. We have a lot of dogs here and are always looking for people who take them on a walk. Your daughter would get the possibility to spend time with the dog without being responsible for it 24/7. Would that be an option?

B: Sounds great! I'll let her know when I get home and I'm sure she will be in. Thanks a lot!

A: Thank you for respecting our conditions and see you soon.

M 2: Homework

a. Allergies, pet owners become sick or die, moving, behavioural problems
b. Shelter should give information on behavioural problems, offer telephone hotlines, educate adopters
c. *Gift*:
- Reason: behavioural problems, the family did not give the dog enough attention, lost their interest
- Prevention: They could have got help from a professional or inform themselves, they probably did not think about their responsibilities before adopting the dog

Bibliography

Dirks, Tim (n.d.). Silent Films. http://www.filmsite.org/silentfilms.html (27/08/2016)

Donaghy, Kieran (2016). The Seven Best Silent Short Films for Language Teaching. http://kierandonaghy.com/seven-best-silent-short-films-language-teaching/ (25/08/2016)

Klepper, Robert (1999). Silent Films, 1877–1996. London: McFarland.

Thaler, Engelbert (2014). Teaching English with Films. Paderborn: Schöningh.

Commercials

Anja Boneberger, Zeynep Direk, Dominik Eberts, Demet Gürsoy

1 Genre

»They have shock, beauty, atmosphere, glamour, drama, comedy, all in the space of 15–30 seconds« (Sherman, cit. in Massler 2006: 135). A commercial, i.e. »a TV spot produced and paid for by an organization, which markets a product, service, or idea,« (Thaler 2014: 75), highlights the qualities of what is being advertised to stimulate the viewers. Some TV commercials do not only seduce them to buy products, but also hint at innovations or problems like poverty and climate change.

As to the structure of commercials, Knoblauch / Raab (2002: 143) distinguish between an *external structure*, which is determined by (television) laws and regulations, and an *internal structure*, which consists of stable and variable attributes. Among the stable attributes there are the »Botschaft des Produktes«, which puts the product itself in the centre, the »Botschaft der Beschreibung«, which focuses on the functions of the product and the attitudes associated with it, and the »*Werbeslogan*«, which may appear at the end of the advertisement.

Concerning different types of commercials, a lot of classifications exist by now. Not few of them derive from Donald Gunn's classic analysis of 12 master formats (www.angelfire.com/linux/audiotrax/12masterformats.html: brief summary, illustrated by sample clips), including the *demo, show the need, symbolize the problem, comparison, exemplary story, testimonial, celebrities*, or *parody*.

The requirements of the two most famous advertising formulae, Lasswell and AIDA, have given rise to recurrent techniques in making commercials, for example surprise effects, intensifiers, scientific evidence, beautiful people, stereotyping, popular songs, jingles, slogans, animation, simplifications, claims, humour, and the overlapping of action with sounds and texts at the same time (Thaler 2014: 75f., Henseler et al 2011: 193).

Numerous arguments speak for integrating commercials into TEFL classrooms (Davis 1997, Henseler et al. 2011, Picken 1999, Rybarczyk 2012, Siegert / Brecheis 2005, Thaler 2014). Children grow up with commercials, as soon as they start watching TV at an early age. TV spots are often intriguing or funny, the topics and situations depicted tie in with students' private lives, sometimes taboos are broken giving rise to controversial discussions, the language frequently aims at »lexikalische Innovation, Modernität, Jugendlichkeit, Sportlichkeit«

(Wyss 1998: 217), and younger learners in particular profit from the repetitive character of commercials. In these products »every word and cinematic device [is] [...] purposeful and precise, which makes them multifaceted objects of analysis« (Thaler 2014: 77). Advertising language is close to everyday speech, but regularly uses stylistic devices such as parallelism, anaphora or rhyme, which are part of most curricula. As commercials often play with stereotypes and clichés, intercultural communicative competence can be developed. Moreover the visuals ease access, facilitate understanding and increase the emotional impact.

Davis (1997) neatly summarizes the TEFL potential of commercials: »Authentic content, short duration, and the combination of words and visual images make commercials the ideal source for innovative, enjoyable and, most importantly, meaningful classroom activities.«

2 Procedure

1st Lesson

Title	The Perfect Getaway (https://www.youtube.com/watch?v=3RgcWidWKhU)
Time	1:12 minutes
Synopsis	The famous actor Pierce Brosnan visits an agent of his, who briefs him about his new role. Brosnan is to star in a car commercial, but he does not know any details yet. The agent successively describes the different scenes of the plot, Brosnan each time expects different twists, and both views are humorously visualised. At the end, Brosnan accepts the role because he can keep the car.
Competences	Viewing, listening, speaking, text and media competence, vocabulary
Topics	Commercial, cars, narration, landscape, opposites, humour
Level	Intermediate
Steps:	

A. Lead-in
T: »Today we are going to study a short film. During the first presentation, however, you won't see the visuals, but only hear the dialogue. Find out what the film is all about.«

B. First screening: vision-off approach
1. The clip is presented with the sound only.
2. S summarize the story-line.
3. T: »What kind of short film is it?«

C. Second screening: stop-and-go approach
1. The clip is presented via stop-and-go technique.
2. Every time the pause button has been pressed, S briefly retell the preceding scene (or describe the freeze frame).

D. Third screening: normal viewing approach
1. The worksheet with the gap-fill exercise is handed out (M 1).
2. The video is shown for the third time.
3. S try to fill in the missing words in the handout.
4. The results are checked in class (via OHP / projector / blackboard).

E. Follow-up
1. Evaluation
   - »Do you like this commercial? Why (not)?«
   - »Do you think it persuades potential customers to buy this car?«
2. Taboo game
In pairs, retell the story of the clip without using the words you filled in the worksheet: *beautiful, car, snowy, road, sniper, a bend, to block, moose, missile launcher, mission, summit, destination, cabin.*

3. (optional) Fantasy trip
Now you are the agent. Tell your own story, come up with new encounters and / or obstacles, or change the ending. Prepare a one-minute talk.

Homework:
Imagine having a nice getaway yourself. Why, when, where would you go and with whom? Next lesson be ready to give a one-minute-talk about your getaway trip.

2nd Lesson

Title	My Dad is a Liar (https://www.youtube.com/watch?v=EZgmj5ay5Bk)
Time	3:26 minutes
Synopsis	In this MetLife commercial, a young girl takes part in an essay competition writing about her father. She describes his personality with several adjectives, mostly positives ones. Their lives seem to be uncomplicated and happy at first sight. Suddenly, a turning point appears in the girl's essay and the video. She starts exhibiting what is hidden below the superficial happiness her dad leads her to believe in. In reality, her father has no permanent white-collar appointment, but works very hard in various menial part-time jobs, and has to cope with lots of obstacles just to make sure that his daughter can go to school and get a good education.
Competences	Listening-viewing, lexis, grammar
Topics	Family, education, role of father, money, economy
Level	Intermediate to advanced

Steps (global-to-detail approach):

1. Lead-in
a. T announces that they are going to see another commercial, which, however, is completely different from the one of the preceding lesson.
b. Class discussion and mind map: »Which adjectives come to your mind when describing a person / father?«

2. First viewing: two sequences (global comprehension)
a. The clip is played till ›but‹-scene (0:53).
b. S give their first impressions of the story:
   – Who writes about whom?
   – How does the life of father and daughter seem to be?
c. T makes S write down the adjectives describing the girl's dad.
d. The video is played to the end.
e. The second part is summarized.
f. Further adjectives describing the father are added.

Lessons

3. Second viewing: straight-through approach (detailed understanding)
a. The video is played a second time.
b. The story is analysed:
   - turning point
   - ending
   - illusion vs reality (the seeming and the real)
c. Authorship and intention are discussed:
   - Who is the producer of this commercial?
   - Why did they produce it?
   - What is your personal attitude to such a strategy?

4. Follow-up
Grammar revision: comparison of adjectives

a. T and S revise the rules of comparison.
b. S find comparative and superlative forms for the adjectives written down in phase 2.

Homework:
»Compare the two commercials: Which do you prefer? Write a blog entry of about 120 words.«

3 Materials

M1:

Worksheet: **The Perfect Getaway**	
Watch the commercial and try to fill in the gaps.	
Agent:	We open on you, driving in a ①_____ ②_____ up a ③_____ ④_____ . … You look up in the trees and you see …«
Pierce:	⑤ a _____ .
Agent:	No, an owl. You come around ⑥_____ , there is something ⑦_____ your way.
Pierce:	A ⑧_____ , right?
Agent:	No, a ⑨_____ .
Pierce:	A ⑨_____ ? Hahaha, why, what's the ⑩_____ ?

Agent:	Oh, there is no ⑩_____ .
Pierce:	Top secret, eh?
Agent:	Yeah, sorta (sort of). So you keep going towards the ⑪_____, your ⑫_____. And there it is, a ⑬_____ .«
Pierce:	A ⑬_____ . And it explodes?
Agent:	What? No, it's just a ⑬_____ .
Pierce:	No explosions?
Agent:	No explosions. But there are fireworks.
Pierce:	Oh, I like fireworks.

4 Solutions

1st Lesson

B. 2: see synopsis.

B. 3: KIA automobile commercial; it promotes the car's abilities to cope with rough mountain conditions.

D: gap-fill exercise
1. beautiful
2. car
3. snowy
4. road
5. sniper
6. a bend
7. to block
8. moose
9. missile launcher
10. mission
11. summit
12. destination
13. cabin

E. 2: Taboo (near-synonyms)

beautiful	elegant, fine, good-looking, gorgeous, stunning, magnificent
car	auto, automobile, jeep, vehicle, SUV
snowy	frosty, wintery, icy, cold
road	roadway, way, route, path, pathway, course, track, trail
sniper	assassin, sharpshooter, killer, marksman
a bend	a corner, a bending, an angle, a turn
to block	to halt, hinder, hold up, impede, intercept, stop
moose	elk (or paraphrasing: large animal)
missile launcher	rocket launcher (or paraphrasing: military vehicle)
mission	quest, duty, job, aim, assignment, objective
summit	top, peak
destination	target, journey's end
cabin	house, lodge, hut

E. 3: fantasy trip
 an avalanche → evasive manoeuvres
 a falling tree → superior brakes
 a snow storm or thick fog → bright headlights
 a collapsing bridge → remarkable acceleration
 a seemingly impossibly steep slope → exceptional grip

2nd Lesson

1.b. Adjectives describing a person: nice, cool, happy, lovely, selfish, tall, big, smart, intelligent ...
Adjectives describing a father: strong, hardworking, patient, funny, friendly, caring ...

2.b. Daughter writes about her father
Life seems to be simple, without any problems. Father and daughter lead ordinary lives like every family. As the mother is not shown, it may be that the father is a single parent. He performs daily routines, taking her daughter to school, going to work, being responsible to earn money. They seem to be very happy and carefree.

2.c. adjectives: sweetest / the most handsome / smartest / the most clever / kindest / great

2.e. After ›but‹, the daughter writes about what her father tries to hide from her, i.e. all his tiresome efforts to make ends meet as he has no proper appointment. He is engaged in different hard jobs just to enable a good education and successful future for his beloved daughter. She is aware of all these problems, feels sorry and is grateful to her wonderful dad.

2.f. other adjectives: tired, hungry

3.c. intention of commercial:
- The commercial has been commissioned by MetLife, an insurance company.
- They want the viewers to get emotionally affected and sign a life insurance contract to care for the future of their offspring. They know that parents' biggest concerns are centred about whether their children have a promising future, a satisfying job, and enough money. A dramatic and shocking video can be an expedient instrument to convince parents to care for their kids' future well-being in the form of a life insurance.
- negative attitude: capitalist manipulation of parents, taking advantage of parents' worries, financially exploiting their feelings of guilt – positive attitude: commercials as indispensable tools of the economy, insurance companies as necessary business branch, making long-term provisions for the sake of the family.

Bibliography

Davis, Randy (1997). TV Commercial Messages: An Untapped Video Resource for Content-Based Classes. In: The Language Teacher Online. http://jalt-publications.org/old_tlt/files/97/mar/davis.html (05.08.2016)

Donaghy, Kieran (2015). Film in Action. Peaslake: Delta Publishing.

Henseler, Roswitha / Möller, Stefan / Surkamp Carola (2011). Filme im Englischunterricht. Seelze: Kallmeyer.

Knoblauch, Hubert / Raab Jürgen (2002). Der Werbespot als Kommunikative Gattung. In: Willems, Herbert (ed.). Die Gesellschaft der Werbung. Kontexte und Texte. Produktion und Rezeptionen. Entwicklungen und Perspektiven. Wiesbaden: Westdeutscher Verlag, pp. 139–154.

Massler, Ute (2006). Adidas, Nike und Pepsi: Football Commercials im Netz und im Fremdsprachenunterricht. In: Thaler, Engelbert (ed.). Fußball – Fremdsprachen – Forschung. Aachen: Shaker Verlag, pp. 135–147.

Picken, Jonathan (1999). State of the Ad: The Role of Advertisements in EFL

Teaching. In: ELT Journal 53 / 4. Oxford: Oxford University Press, pp. 249–255.
Rybarczyk, Renate (2012). Zum Einsatz von Kurzfilmen im Fremdsprachenunterricht am Beispiel von Werbespots. In: Zeitschrift für Interkulturellen Fremdsprachenunterricht. Darmstadt: Sprachenzentrum der TU Darmstadt, pp. 143–156.
Siegert, Gabriele / Brecheis, Dieter (2005). Werbung in der Medien- und Informationsgesellschaft. Wiesbaden: Verlag für Sozialwissenschaften.
Thaler, Engelbert (2014). Teaching English with Films. Paderborn: Ferdinand Schöningh. http://www.angelfire.com/linux/audiotrax/12masterformats.html

Animated Shorts

Susanne Klohn

1 Genre

»Animated movies displayed via computers is one of the modern methods of education that works on activating the child's imagination, educates him [or her] and entertains him [or her]« (Eman / Naglaa 2010: 367). The term *animation* derives from the Latin verb *animare*, i.e. ›to give life to‹, and within the context of the animated film, this refers to the artificial creation of the illusion of movement in inanimate lines and forms (Wells 1998: 10).

The history of the animated film begins in the early 20th century with two men who were drawing comics for a newspaper, before they started to experiment with animation (Smith 1977: 23). Stuart Blackton started giving so-called *chalk-talks*, something like slow-motion animation, and his 1906 film record of one of these talks called *Humorous Phases of Funny Faces* is usually considered the first animated film (Smith 1977: 23f.). The first full animated film was *Little Nemo* in 1911, whose creator is also responsible for the first colour cartoon (Wells 1998: 16).

Today, animation films are an important and successful film genre, especially for a younger audience. However, they are not only meant for children, as the topics vary considerably, ranging from simple and funny films for pure entertainment to serious and difficult ones, for example the short films *Endless* and *Father And Daughter*. »Of all the many short films used in high school classes, cartoons and animated films may be the most provocative. Students accustomed to thinking of cartoons or animated films as pure entertainment – something Disney carried to its logical items – are often surprised to discover that these films can convey serious reflections and ideas about modern man and the problems in his modern world« (Doleson 1972: 157).

Furthermore, Champoux (2001: 81) lists a few reasons why animated shorts are very valuable teaching material:

- The visualization can create strong, lasting images of concepts.
- Animation offers alternatives to live-action scenes, which increases variety in the classroom.
- Exaggeration helps link abstract concepts to visual symbols.
- Borrowing from Roger Ebert's observation, animations can help us link concepts directly to the mind of our students.

2 Procedure

Title	The Present
Synopsis	A teenage boy is playing video games when his mother arrives with a present: a puppy. The boy is delighted, until he sees the dog's disability: one leg is missing. He abandons him, but the dog still enjoys playing with a ball and a box in a very clumsy but life-affirming manner, making the teenager smile. Finally the dog's positive attitude convinces the boy to play with his new companion. When the boy gets up, the reason for his initial reluctance is seen: he also has only one leg. At the end, he goes outside and plays with the dog, visibly in a happier mood than before.
Competences	Speaking, writing, listening-viewing
Topics	Disability, teenagers, computer games, pets
Level	Intermediate
Time	2 x 45 minutes

Steps: Lesson 1

A. Pre-viewing stage
1. Teacher (T) tells the students (S) that they are going to watch an animated short film.
2. T asks what kinds of animated films S have seen and what they know about the genre.
3. T tells S the name of the film and asks them what the film may be about.

B. While-viewing stage
1. a) T shows film until 00:06: Only a black screen is seen and war sounds can be heard.
b) S guess again what the film is about and describe the scenery they expect to see.
2. a) T shows film until 00:51: The mother has brought in the present and the boy is about to open it.
b) Everyone writes down one or two ideas about the content of the box.
c) S share their ideas and discuss reasons for them.
3. a) T shows film until 1:21: The boy reacts to the dog's handicap in a very negative manner, throwing him down to the floor and kicking him away.
b) S describe the teenager's reaction and discuss possible reasons for his behaviour.
c) S are asked to predict a possible ending of the film.
4. a) T shows film until 02:45: the boy has changed his mind and smiles at the dog.
b) S try to figure out the reason for this change, also guessing what may happen next.

5. a) T shows the rest of the film, revealing the unexpected ending, which displays the boy's own handicap.
b) S talk about their feelings and discuss the message of the film.

C. Post-viewing: Think-pair-share
1. T hands out worksheet (M1: The boy's thoughts).
2. Individually, S fill in the thought bubbles before and after the boy has changed his mind.
3. S get together with a partner and exchange their thoughts.
4. The results are collected in class.

Homework:
Summarize this animated film in a few sentences.

Lesson 2

A. Revision
1. S read out their homework.
2. Other S give feedback, adding or discarding pieces of information.
3. A few guiding questions may help S remember the most important facts.
- What did the boy do at the beginning?
- Why did he stop playing?
- What happened when the boy first saw the dog?
- Why did the boy treat the dog badly at the beginning?
- What happened to change his mind?
- How did the story end?

B. Group work
1. S get together in six groups.
2. As there are three topics, two groups get the same topic (M 2).
3. Realia which are supposed to arouse S's imagination are given to the groups:
- item 1: two old mobile phones
- item 2: a video still of the disabled dog
- item 3: a toy dog
4. The groups make notes and prepare their dialogues.
5. The results are acted out.
6. The other groups give feedback on the content and the language.
7. T adds comments and summarizes the presentation phase.

Homework
S have to write down (complete) the dialogue in their exercise books, which will be collected by the T the following lesson.

3 Materials

M1: The boy's thoughts
   Animated Short Film: »The Present«

Source: https://www.youtube.com/watch?v=96kI8Mp1uOU. Time 01:17 and 03:03

M 2: Group exercise

Group 1
The mother is worried about her son's mental state, deriving from his disability. She calls her friend and talks about possible ideas to make him feel better and get out more often. Write a dialogue, which ends with the idea of buying a dog.
Roles: mother, friend, narrator introducing the situation

Group 2
The boy's mother thinks about buying the disabled dog for her son. She argues with the other parent, who is against this kind of present.
Roles: Mother, other parent, narrator introducing the situation

Group 3
The boy tells his best friend Mary about his day with the puppy, including his first impression, how he changed his mind and what his day with the dog was like. Mary is interested and asks a lot of questions.
Roles: Boy, best friend, narrator introducing the situation

4 Solutions

M1: The boy's thoughts (one pupil's answer)
At the beginning:
My mum is making fun of me, just like everyone else! Such a stupid dog, crippled like me. He is disgusting! He reminds me of my own disability and I hate it! Nobody wants such a dog or such a friend. I am so angry, my mother always wants me to be okay with my leg, but I'm not, I hate it! And this dog is the same and reminds me of it! I'll tell her to throw it out when she comes back!

At the end:
Maybe it's not that bad to be handicapped. It doesn't mean that I can't have fun anymore. This puppy also misses one leg, but he's lively and happy as any other puppy. And it's so much fun watching him play. He will be a good friend for me, I am sure. He already helps me open the door! Now I have a reason to go out again and probably all my friends want to play with my dog, too.

Guiding questions (2nd lesson, revision)

- What did the boy do at the beginning?
  He was playing video games, sitting on the sofa in the dark living-room with all the blinds shut.

- Why did he stop playing?
  The mother came home, opened the blinds and placed a present on the table in front of the boy, telling him that the present is for him. As he wanted to open it he stopped playing.
- What happened when the boy first saw the dog?
  He was delighted until he saw the disability.
- Why did the boy treat the dog badly at the beginning?
  After he saw the injury he abandoned the dog. At that moment of the film, the reason for the boy's behaviour is left open, but at the end of the film, the boy's handicap becomes visible. He does not want the dog, because he suffers from his own disability and does not want to be reminded of it, or displays his self-hatred in the behaviour towards the dog.
- What happened to change his mind?
  He sees that the dog is not bothered by the disability, but seems happy and lively. He does not give up, but enjoys playing and living, which reminds the boy that his life could be similar.
- How did the story end?
  The boy goes outside to play with the dog and is likely to be happier than before.

M2: Possible solutions for group tasks
Group 1 (one student's answer)
Introduction: Billy's mother Cassie is worried about her son. He never goes out and hardly has any friends. He sits in the living-room all day, playing video games, after he had the accident where he lost his leg. Cassie calls her best friend Bob asking for advice.

Bob:	Hey Cassie, how are you? Nice to be hearing from you.
Cassie:	Hey Bob, I'm not very well today. I'm really worried about my son Billy. Since he had this accident, he is not the same person anymore. He just hides inside, doesn't meet any friends and hardly goes out. I don't know what to do about it.
Bob:	Hm, I'm sorry to hear that. I know, it's not easy for your son, since he was a good football player and had a lot of friends in the football club. Maybe he just needs more time?
Cassie:	It's already three months now since he got out of the hospital! I would really love to see him smile again and go out, life is not lost just because he only has one leg now.

Bob:	I know, I know, I think he needs something that drags him out a bit. What about a new club where he doesn't need his leg? Maybe swimming or archery or something.
Cassie:	No, I already talked to him about it. He doesn't want to do anything else.
Bob:	Hm, what about travelling with him?
Cassie:	Good idea, but I have to work a lot right now, I can't travel now. I need to give him something that helps him enjoy his life again.
Bob:	Oh, now I have a great idea: what about buying a dog for him? He would be forced to go out and a pet always makes life happier.
Cassie:	What a marvellous idea! Yeah, a dog would be such a good present for him! Tomorrow I'll go to the pet shop and look for a puppy for him. Thanks, Bob, you are the best!
Bob:	Ah, Cassie, I'm always glad to help you. Call me and tell me how he reacted!
Cassie:	Oh, yes, I will! See you, Bob!
Bob:	Bye!

Group 2 (one student's answer)

Introduction: Billy's mother Cassie had the idea to buy a dog for her son, who lost a leg in an accident some months ago, and since then doesn't go out anymore and becomes more and more depressed. She went to the pet shop and saw a nice little puppy with also only one leg. She thinks this is the perfect present for her son, but wants to talk about it with her husband Kyle first.

Cassie:	Hey honey. I had a great idea to fight Billy's depression!
Kyle:	Really? Wow, I would love to hear about it!
Cassie:	I thought about getting him a dog, so he has to go outside again and has something to be glad about.
Kyle:	Great idea, I think that will help a lot!
Cassie:	Yeah, I know, and I already went to the pet shop and found the perfect puppy!
Kyle:	Oh great! Do you have a picture?
Cassie:	Yes, here it is! Isn't he nice? *(shows him the picture of the puppy with only three legs)*
Kyle:	Oh ... I don't think that this is a good idea, honey.

Cassie:	Why not? He will like him, because they are alike.
Kyle:	No, I think he will hate him, because he hates what happened to himself and hasn't accepted his own disability yet. He will probably abandon him.
Cassie:	I don't think so. You haven't seen the puppy, he is so lively and enjoys playing around and ...
Kyle:	Billy will think we want to make fun of him ...
Cassie:	No way! Maybe he will not like him when he first sees him, but as soon as he sees him playing around and having so much fun, not being bothered by his missing leg at all, he will see that life can go on and that it is still wonderful, even if you are disabled.
Kyle:	Hm, you've got a point there. Maybe you are right.
Cassie:	I saw the dog, he is really joyful and will cheer Billy up.
Kyle:	Don't you think that the other kids will make fun of him with this dog?
Cassie:	I think that he will protect his puppy from the others' laughter and so he will learn not to be bothered by it himself. I think it will all go well.
Kyle:	Okay, then let's try it. If he doesn't like him, we have to give him back, but it's worth a try, I guess.
Cassie:	Great! Then I'll go and get the dog tomorrow!
Kyle:	Okay. I'm really keen to see what happens!

Group 3 (one student's answer)

Introduction: Billy hasn't gone out since days. This morning, he has received a present from his mother. It is a dog with only three legs. Billy is also missing a leg, so first he doesn't like the dog, but later plays with him and really enjoys the day outside. In the evening, his best friend Mary visits him and Billy tells her about his day.

Mary:	Hey Billy, how are you?
Billy:	Hey Mary! I'm great! Look at this! *(He takes the dog and shows it to Mary)*
Mary:	Wow! What a lovely little fellow! *(She pets the dog)* Where did you get it from?
Billy:	My mother gave it to me today! Isn't he really cute?
Mary:	Oh, yes, he is. What's his name?
Billy:	Marshmallow.

Mary:	Oh, what a cute name! But what about this leg?
Billy:	Yeah, it's missing. I know, first, I really thought my mum wants to make fun of me, buying a disabled dog.
Mary:	Oh, I don't think she would do that!
Billy:	No, I know now, but when I saw him, I hated him, because he was disabled like me and I hate my own disability. But then he played around and had so much fun that I really couldn't look away.
Mary:	Yeah, I can imagine, puppies are very lively. Did you change your mind then?
Billy:	Oh yes. And while he was having so much fun, he didn't even care about his missing leg. When he fell, he stood up again, just over and over again, he wasn't even angry about it.
Mary:	Mhm, he enjoys life! And then, what did you do?
Billy:	I couldn't hate him anymore, it was just so much fun watching him play! So I went out!
Mary:	Really? You haven't been out for a long time!
Billy:	I know, but then we played in the garden the whole day, he didn't get tired and I always had to go after him. It was so much fun!
Mary:	How do you feel now?
Billy:	I'm really tired and my arms hurt, I haven't moved so much for a very long time, but I feel great!
Mary:	Whoa, that's great! I'm really happy for you. Are you going to go out with him again tomorrow?
Billy:	Yes, for sure! He needs a lot of running and playing! Do you want to come with us?
Mary:	Yes, of course! I'll visit you tomorrow at 11 a.m., is that okay?
Billy:	I need to go out with him early, but we'll be back at about nine, I think, and then we can go out again at 11. So, okay!
Mary:	Cool, then see you tomorrow! And you, little Marshmallow!
Billy:	See you!

Bibliography

Champoux, Joseph E. 2001. »Animated Films As a Teaching Material.« Journal of Management Education, Vol. 25 No. 1. 79–100.

Eman, A. A. & Naglaa, F. K. 2010. »Effectiveness of an Educational Program via Anmated Movies.« World Journal of Sport Sciences, 3. 359–376.

Donelsen, Kenneth L. 1972. »Cartoons and Animated Films Disney Wouldn't Have Made: Five Provocative Short Films.« The High School Journal, Vol 55, No. 4. 157–161.

Smith, Conrad. 1977. »The Early History of Animation.« Journal of the University Film Association, XXIX, 3. 23–30.

Wells, Paul. 1998. Understanding Animation. Abingdon: Routledge.

Infrographic Films

Susanne Neumann

1 Genre

An infographic is a visual representation of information, data or knowledge intended to present facts quickly and clearly (Thaler 2015). It can improve cognition by utilizing graphics to enhance the ability of the human visual system to see patterns and trends (Knieper 1995: 3f.). Since the 1980s, infographics have gone a step beyond traditional graphics (charts, timelines, tables, graphs) by connecting mostly numeric content with appealing design. Related data sets are linked into a unified, visually compelling representation relating a more complex story (Krauss 2012: 10).

Infographic films, also referred to as videographics, are animated infographics, which are usually between two and five minutes long. The mixture of animated drawings, graphs or tables is mostly accompanied by an audio track and intends to convey information about a specific topic or a complex issue. The audio gives further information and contextualizes the visuals. Some videographics, however, do without audio as they are self-explanatory through the graphs and images displayed.

There are several reasons why videographics should be integrated into the modern EFL classroom. They represent authentic material students are familiar with as they have become popular on TV and online for conveying information in an aesthetically appealing and understandable way. »There is a special thrill in being able to understand and enjoy the real thing« (Sherman 2003: 2). Thanks to online platforms like YouTube or Vimeo and TV news in English-speaking TV channels, a great variety of infographic films is easily accessible and for free. As they treat current political, economic and social issues they are well suited for intercultural and global learning. Moreover Paivio's dual-coding theory suggests that the combination of pictures and short texts or figures increases the possibility to transfer knowledge to the long-term memory (Paivio 1986: 53f), so that the chance to recall a piece of information is higher as the individual can retrieve it from both verbal and visual channels instead of a single one. The study of discontinuous texts such as printed graphs and statistics has already become an established feature in TEFL curricula, so the modern audio-visual successors like infographic films should also be included in teaching.

Videographics can transform complicated issues into digestible, visually compelling short films through motion graphics and digital media. It should, however, not be ignored that »the real thing« can be quite challenging as videographics tend to be presented very fast and bristle with facts, which may lead to information overload.

2 Procedure

Lesson 1

Title	Fast Food Business – Shocking Truth Behind It (www.youtube.com/watch?v=tyVFGpg17hw)
Synopsis	This infographic film (2 minutes 15 seconds) presents numerous facts and statistics about the fast food industry, e.g. the number of restaurants, people's eating habits, the economic power of fast food companies, the average daily calorie intake per country, or the relationship between obesity and death.
Competences	Listening-viewing, speaking, intercultural communicative competence, text competence (infographics as genre), vocabulary
Topics	Fast food business in the US, economy, eating habits
Level	Lower intermediate – intermediate
Time	45 minutes

Steps (10-Step Approach to Listening-Viewing)

1. Listening-viewing motivation
a) T: »Let's have a guess: What vegetable do Americans eat most?«
b) S come up with individual answers.
c) T: »We'll find out in a minute which of you is right.«

2. Preparatory work
a) Via brainstorming on fast food, relevant vocabulary on fast food is collected in a board sketch.
b) T adds new words, e.g. food ad(vertisement), average daily calorie intake, obesity, diet.

3. First viewing purpose
S watch the video guided by three questions:
a) What vegetable do Americans eat most?
b) In what form is it consumed?
c) How many fast food restaurants can be found in the US?

4. First viewing
The video is played straight through.

5. Comprehension
a) The three questions (3.a/b/c) are answered.
b) T additionally presents a few true / false statements for S.
 - »McDonalds was the first fast food company in the US.«
 - »Most potatoes are consumed as French fries.«
 - »20 % of Americans eat fast food every day.«
 - »More than half of the customers buy via drive-through.«
 - »Fast food chains do not spend much money on advertising.«
 - »McDonalds has restaurants in every country of the world.«

6. Second viewing purpose
S are asked to pay attention to the way the facts are presented.

7. Second viewing
The whole video is presented again.

8. Analysis
T has taken screenshots from the film which help him / her to introduce S to the techniques of infographics (M 1). T and S fill in the worksheet together and discuss how information is conveyed in infographic films, using appropriate register.

9. (optional): Third viewing
If time allows, the clip may be played again for better understanding.

10. Wrap up
a) Discussion: In groups of three S discuss fast food:
  - Why is too much fast food bad for us?
  - What does a healthy diet look like?
  - Is it possible / necessary to do without fast food?
b) Nutrition pyramid (M 2): S explain what a healthy and balanced diet should look like: »Which products do you see in the nutrition pyramid, and in which quantities should you eat them?«

Lesson 2

Title	What's Trending @ Twitter (https://www.youtube.com/watch?v=r__UEFT0hPk)
Synopsis	This videographic (2 minutes 22 seconds) presents a study of Twitter users, conducted by Lab 42, to see how people use the service, what they use it for, why they have joined Twitter, how they find followers, or what celebrities they follow. The particularity of this video is that there is no spoken text added to the images, which are self-explanatory as they feature all numbers and results in written text form.
Competences	Listening-viewing, media competence (usage and attitudes towards social media), text competence (form and function of videographics), speaking
Topics	Social media, Twitter, technology, celebrities
Level	Upper-intermediate
Time	45–90 minutes

Steps (pre – while – post approach)

A. Pre-viewing
a) S fill in a survey about their usage of social media (M 1). The handouts may be collected, analysed and discussed in one of the following lessons. Alternatively, a few answers may be called upon in class.
b) The differences between traditional charts and videographics are discussed. For reasons of clarity and illustration, T may present one example each via OHP or handout.

B. While-viewing
a) A worksheet with tasks for global and detailed understanding is handed out and explained (M 2).
b) The video is shown for the first time.
c) Global understanding is checked orally.
d) The class is divided into three groups: Group A is supposed to focus on content, B on formal representation, C on cinematic techniques (see questions on worksheet).
e) The three groups present their results and get feedback from the others.

C. Post-viewing
Expert interview (role play, jigsaw technique): An interviewer asks an IT graphic designer as well as a social media professor about the role of infographics.
a) The three roles are allocated to the S.
b) In the three expert groups, questions or statements are prepared.
c) Then S leave their expert groups and mingle with the representatives of the other roles, so that in each group there is one interviewer, one designer and one professor.
d) A few interviews may be presented in front of the whole class.

D. Homework
S are asked to find an infographic film related to a topic they are interested in. They should be prepared to show the film the following lesson and explain why they like it.

3 Materials

Lesson 1

M 1: Infographics

Infographic films or *videograhics* are a mixture of animated drawings, graphs and tables, which are often accompanied by an audio track. They convey information about specific topics or complex issues in a simple way.

Example	Term	Function
	Chronological **timeline**	• temporal overview • structure
	icons / **pictograms**	Illustration, less text, → better understanding
	facts and **figures**	• preciseness • scientific appearance

Infographic films or *videograhics* are a mixture of animated drawings, graphs and tables, which are often accompanied by an audio track. They convey information about specific topics or complex issues in a simple way.		
Example	Term	Function
	bar chart	• survey results • display of relationships
	pie chart and **percentages**	• survey results • relationships
	photos / realia	• link to real life • authenticity • illustration
	logos and **brand names**	• link to real life • exemplification • advertising • criticizing

M 2: Food pyramid

http://florette.de/wpcontent/uploads/2015/12/Ern%C3%A4hrungspyramide.jpg

Lesson 2

M 1: Survey

Social Media Usage – a Short Survey

Answer the following questions honestly, please.

Which social media platforms do you currently use?

☐ Facebook	☐ Pinterest	☐ Vimeo	☐ Other: _____
☐ YouTube	☐ Instagram	☐ Flickr	
☐ Snapchat	☐ Twitter	☐ LinkedIn	

How many hours do you spend on average on these platforms per day?

☐ Less than 30 minutes	☐ 2–3h
☐ 30 min – 1h	☐ 3–4h
☐ 1–2h	☐ More than 4 hours

What functions do you use most?

☐ Chatting	☐ Checking out other people's profiles	☐ Other
☐ Writing longer messages	☐ Commenting	
☐ Watching videos	☐ Posting	

Give reasons why you use them?

☐ To stay connected with friends ☐ To post about my life ☐ Other

☐ To entertain myself ☐ To follow celebrities and trends

☐ To communicate with friends ☐ To portray myself online

Are you familiar with the privacy policy and practices of the platforms where you are registered?

☐ No, not at all ☐ I am well informed about them

☐ A little bit ☐ I am not interested in that

☐ Roughly

M 2: Twitter Worksheet

Videographic – What's Trending @ Twitter
(https://www.youtube.com/watch?v=r__UEFT0hPk)

A. Global understanding
Watch the videographic without taking notes and answer the following questions orally. 1. Summarize the topic of the videographic in one sentence.
2. Recall one piece of information / one detail that surprised you most?

B. Detailed understanding
Watch the video for a second time. Pay particular attention to the tasks your group has to focus on. Take notes as you are going to present your findings to the other groups.

Group A: Focus on content
1. What pieces of information are given?
2. In what order are they presented?
Group B: Focus on formal representation
1. What graphic forms are used to depict the results?
2. How are certain results highlighted?

Group C: Focus on cinematic techniques
1. How would you describe the sound?
2. What editing techniques do you recognize?

C. Jigsaw role play

Imagine being in an interview about social media usage and videographics. One of you is the graphic designer of the videographic you have just seen, the other is a lecturer teaching digital communication at Steinhart's University for Media and Communication, New York, the third is the interviewer.

- Interviewer: Think of questions you might like to ask the IT graphic designer and the media researcher.
- Media lecturer: You could talk about the developments with regard to social media usage among young adults and about the biggest (dis-)advantages of Facebook & Co.
- Graphic designer: You may talk about the potential of animated infographics and about the difficulty to simplify complex topics for the mainstream user.

Prepare the interview and act it out in groups of three.

3 Solutions

Lesson 1

2. Board sketch

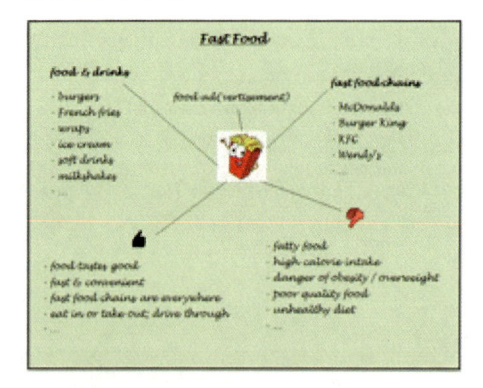

Fast Food

food & drinks
- burgers
- french fries
- wraps
- ice cream
- soft drinks
- milkshakes

food ad (advertisement)

fast food chains
- McDonalds
- Burger King
- KFC
- Wendy's

👍
- food tastes good
- fast & convenient
- fast food chains are everywhere
- eat in or take out; drive through

👎
- fatty food
- high calorie intake
- danger of obesity / overweight
- poor quality food
- unhealthy diet

5.a) Questions
   a) potato
   b) French fries

c) 160,000
5.b) True (T) / False (F):
F – T – F – T – F – F

Lesson 2

M 2: Twitter Worksheet
A.1. The videographic presents the results of a survey in which Twitter users were asked about their usage habits.
A.2. e.g. »The most followed celebrity on Twitter is Barack Obama.«

B. Group A
1. Number of brands a user follows, reasons why users follow others ...
2. Frequency of use, forms of access, quantity of use, reasons to join, people one follows

Group B
1. Lists, bar charts, pie charts, photos, written text, numbers
2. The highest percentages are highlighted with the Twitter bird; different colours and forms are used to emphasize specific survey results.

Group C
1. Sound: electronic music, endless tune, occasional typing sounds
2. Editing: gradual development of the frames, many fade-ins and fade-outs (pictures, texts), wipe (clouds cover the previous image) creating fluidity

C: Interviewer
   Questions to the professor:

- »Can you report about current social media trends which you have observed recently?«
- »What kind of long-term effect can social media have?«
- »Are we getting more connected or even less as the number of contacts exceeds our time to take care of them?«

Questions to the graphic designer:

- »What is the most challenging part when creating videographics?«
- »Where do you find inspiration for new forms, designs and ways to convey messages?«

Media professor
   »We have observed that the latest social media platforms tend to become more and more specialized. Services such as Instagram or Snapchat focus on

one single function (photos, films). The usage becomes simpler and the posting process quicker. Due to this acceleration, we have recognized changes with regard to the users' attention span.« ...

Graphic designer
»As a graphic designer, you have an eye for forms and trends. You scan logos, advertisements and everything else that features some kind of design. Through this constant observation, you shape your idea of progressive designs and form.«

»With regard to videographics, the most difficult part is to anticipate what the viewer already knows and what he does not know. Sometimes, I feel like a teacher who needs to choose what comes first. Often, we get bulks of information for a project and we only use a fraction of them for the final video. Then the design is the easier part most of the time.«

Bibliography

Knieper, Thomas. 1995. Infographiken: Das visuelle Informationspotential der Tageszeitung. München: Verlag Reinhard Fischer.

Krauss, Jane. 2012. »More Than Words Can Say. Infographics«. In: Learning & Leading with Technology. URL: http://files.eric.ed.gov/fulltext/EJ982831.pdf (last accessed August 12, 2016).

Paivio, Allan. 1986. Mental Representations. A Dual Coding Approach. New York: OUP.

Sherman, Jane. 2003. Using Authentic Video in the Language Classroom. Cambridge: Cambridge University Press.

Thaler, Engelbert. 2015. »Das geht ins Auge – Visualisierung mit Infografiken.« Praxis Fremdsprachenunterricht, 06/15, 12–15.

Social Shorts

Lea Mittelstädt, Maria Sachsinger, Linda Ringwald

1 Genre

Social shorts are short films that deal with social topics, e.g. discrimination, poverty, homelessness, violence, migration. They look at the »world that surrounds us« or »life that we live« from a critical and often delicate point of view. Quite often charities, NGOs (Non-Governmental Organisations) or supra-/international organisations like UNICEF commission them to raise viewers' awareness of a certain social, economic or political problem.

Ambitious filmmakers can send in their products to established short film festivals such as the International Festival of Social Short-Films in Barcelona (13th festival in 2017, categories: fiction, documentary), or the AACTA's (Australian Academy Cinema Television Arts) national online short film competition, which devotes three weeks to social shorts, providing emerging Australian filmmakers with the opportunity to have their work seen and acknowledged by film enthusiasts and the screen industry (three categories: comedy, drama, open).

Donaghy (2015: 26) points out that as they often treat issues relating to students' lives, social shorts are very gripping, dramatic and emotional. »This fosters learner engagement and enthusiasm to communicate« (Ib.).

2 Procedure

Title	How do you turn a life around? (https://www.youtube.com/watch?v=3xGkNBerxe0)
Time	1:53 minutes
Synopsis	»Every child deserves a fair chance in life« (UNICEF). Unfortunately, millions of children suffer from being left behind, disadvantaged and deprived. This UNICEF video shows the contrast between children who have the opportunity to live a happy life and others who are forced to do hard work, are abused and mistreated. It is divided into four scenes, which highlight the contrasts in living conditions. The clip ends by calling upon viewers to help UNICEF: »Every child deserves a fair chance in life. Join us to FightUnfair.«

Competences	Listening-viewing, speaking, intercultural communicative competence, grammar (gerund), vocabulary
Topics	Child poverty, injustice, Unicef, giving donations, contrasts: outdoor games vs child labour, compliment vs rebuke, respect vs disdain, pleasure vs struggle for life
Level	Intermediate

Steps:
A. Pre-viewing stage
1. From the title of the video, S speculate about the content of it.
2. T: »What do you know about different lifestyles of children? Does everyone have the same chances and rights?«
3. »Have a guess: How many children worldwide are engaged in child labour?« (UNICEF: 150 million)

B. While-viewing stage: four parts (freeze frames)
1. First freeze frame after the first scene (00:08): »How could their lives change to the negative?«
2. After the second scene (00:31): »What could be different?«
3. After the third scene (00:52): »Can you imagine the situation being worse?«
4. After the fourth scene (01:16): »In this scene the kids are playing very peacefully. Nevertheless, there are children who struggle for life and survival. How could the video continue? Think of a concrete example.«
5. After the end: »Compare your predictions with the real ending.«
6. The final text in the clip says: »Every child deserves a fair chance in life. Join us to FightUnfair.« S are asked to comment on these last words.

C. Post-viewing stage
a. One of the YouTube comments reads: »Don't give a brass penny to these twats ... They spend all your donations on non-stop annoying TV commercials and the fatcat bosses' salary and lifestyle.« Say whether you agree with this critical statement.
b. Grammar revision: The gerund
   – T may repeat form and function of gerunds briefly.
   – Worksheet (M2) is handed out, and the tasks are read out:
   – »Try to find a heading for each picture.«
   – »Match the appropriate verbs with the scenes and make a sentence using a gerund.«

D. Homework
S are asked to write a text about the prevention of child labour from the point of view of an aid organisation by using gerund constructions (about 100 words).

Lessons

3 Materials

M1: How do you turn a life around?

First try to find a heading for each picture. Then choose an appropriate verb for each scene, and make a sentence by using the gerund.

to appreciate – to enjoy – to risk – to admit – to avoid – to advise – to escape

1. _____
Example:

2. _____
Example:

3. _____
Example:

4. _____
Example:

4 Solutions

M1:
a. Outdoor activities for children
   Example: The boys enjoy playing in the sand.
b. Physical abuse
   Example: The father avoids talking calmly to his son.
c. A school day in an African classroom
   Example: The pupil appreciates giving a talk.
d. Refugees struggle for life
   Example: The children risk dying during the dangerous journey.

Bibliography

Donaghy, Kieran (2015). Film in Action. Peaslake: Delta Publishing.

Viral Shorts

Lea Mittelstädt, Maria Sachsinger, Linda Ringwald

1 Genre

The ascendency of email, film-sharing websites (YouTube or Vimeo), and social media (Facebook or Twitter), has created new types of clips such as the *viral short*. The term refers to any type of short film which becomes very popular through being shared quickly and widely on the Internet. It reaches millions of people after a few days of being shown for the first time, spreads like a wildfire or virus – hence it »goes viral«.

O'Neill (2011) points out four factors contributing to a video becoming viral:

- Viewership: According to Kevin Nalty, a co-blogger of hers, a video is »viral« if it gets more than 5 million views in a 3–7 day period.
- Buzz: The degree of discussion online and offline is high; however, the cause – effect relationship is touched on here since the viral nature of a video prompts coverage, which inspires even more views.
- Parody: Imitation means flattery, and when people copy, remix, and re-create a video, it must be a hit.
- Longevity: The video is remembered for a long time, so it stands the test of time.

The language classroom can benefit from the use of viral shorts through these features. As they are very popular on social media, chances are that students will also find them interesting. Viral videos »are often funny, strange or powerful« (Donaghy 2015: 26), so learners ...

- react strongly to them,
- like discussing how they make them feel,
- enjoy writing critiques of them.

2 Procedure

Title	Look Up http://garyturk.com/portfolio-item/lookup/ (4 minutes 59 seconds)
Synopsis	This spoken word film, which was written, performed and directed by Gary Turk, is addressed to an online generation. Through a love story, it shows us a world where we incessantly find ways that make it easier to connect with other people, but in fact we always spend more time alone. People become unsocial by using social media, and they miss a lot of chances in real life. Ironically, although this video encourages people to look up from their phones, and cut down their use of social media, it has gone viral. On 21 December 2016 it already had 26,623,211 views on Youtube, and it had only gone up at the end of April 2016.
Competences	Viewing, speaking, literary communicative competence (analysing poems), intercultural learning, creative writing, grammar
Topics	Social media, cell phones, isolation, reality vs. illusion, modern society
Level	Advanced
Time	90 minutes

Steps (PWP approach):

A. Pre-viewing
1. Poem *Look up* by Gary Turk: T shows first line on transparency (M1) as a *silent impulse* and hopes for S's reactions.
2. T uncovers the second line: »What could be the overall topic?«
3. T shows lines 3 and 4: »What problem is meant here?«
4. T shows lines 5–8: »What contrast is criticised here?«
5. Think-pair-share: »What are problems of social media?«
6. T introduces a few key words: *companionship – delusion – greedy – to exaggerate – glistening – insane – distraction*

B. While-viewing
1. The worksheet (M 2) is handed out and briefly explained.
2. The video is presented.
3. The questions on the worksheet are discussed.

C. Post- viewing
1. T hands out the text of the whole poem (M 3).
2. S are asked to read the poem silently and find a title for it.
3. The message of the poem is discussed in class.
4. Evaluation of the viral nature of the video:
a) »Why, do you think, has this video gone viral, i.e. become so popular?«
b) »Who does the film appeal to?«
c) »Would you like to share this video?«

Homework
S can choose between two options:
a) Creative writing: »Give people your love, don't give them your like«. Based on this quote, write a short script for your own video, in which you want to convince other teenagers to »look up«.
b) Repetition of grammar (conditional sentences, type 3): Write seven sentences according to the pattern »What would have happened to the young man in the video if ...«

3 Materials

M 1: Transparency

(1) I have 422 friends, yet I am lonely.
(2) I speak to all of them every day, yet none of them really know me.
(3) The problem I have sits in the spaces between,
(4) Looking into their eyes, or at a name on a screen.
(5) I took a step back, and opened my eyes,
(6) I looked around, and then realised
(7) That this media we call social, is anything but
(8) When we open our computers, and it's our doors we shut

M 2: Worksheet

First watch the video, and then answer the questions.
1. Name the disadvantages of social media.
2. What was the situation of the narrator like when he was a child? What is different now?
3. What can life be like if you do not use the mobile all the time?
4. Fill in the gaps in the following lines from the video:

Don't give in to a _____ where you follow the hype,
Give people your _____, don't give them your _____.
Disconnect from the need to be heard and defined
Go out into the _____, leave distractions behind.
_____, shut down that _____,
Stop watching this _____, live life the _____.

5. How would you summarize the intention of this video-poem?

M 3: Poem

_____ (by Gary Turk)

I have 422 friends, yet I am lonely.
I speak to all of them every day, yet none of them really know me.

The problem I have sits in the spaces between,
looking into their eyes, or at a name on a screen.

I took a step back, and opened my eyes,
I looked around, and then realised
that this media we call social, is anything but
when we open our computers, and it's our doors we shut.

All this technology we have, it's just an illusion,
of community, companionship, a sense of inclusion
yet when you step away from this device of delusion,
you awaken to see, a world of confusion.

A world where we're slaves to the technology we mastered,
where our information gets sold by some rich greedy bastard.

A world of self-interest, self-image, self-promotion,
where we share all our best bits, but leave out the emotion.

We are at our most happy with an experience we share,
but is it the same if no one is there.
Be there for you friends, and they'll be there too,
but no one will be, if a group message will do.

We edit and exaggerate, we crave adulation,
we pretend we don't notice the social isolation.
We put our words into order, until our lives are glistening,
we don't even know if anyone is listening.

Being alone isn't the problem, let me just emphasize,
that if you read a book, paint a picture, or do some exercise,
you are being productive, and present, not reserved or recluse,
you're being awake and attentive, and putting your time to good use.

So when you're in public, and you start to feel alone,
put your hands behind your head, and step away from the phone.
You don't need to stare at your menu, or at your contact list,
just talk to one another, and learn to co-exist.

I can't stand to hear the silence, of a busy commuter train,
when no one wants to talk through the fear of looking insane.
We're becoming unsocial, it no longer satisfies
to engage with one another, and look into someone's eyes.

We're surrounded by children, who since they were born,
watch us living like robots, and think it's the norm.
It's not very likely you will make world's greatest dad,
if you cant entertain a child without a using an iPad.

When I was a child, I would never be home,
I'd be out with my friends, on our bikes we would roam.
We'd ware holes in our trainers, and graze up our knees;
we'd build our own clubhouse, high up in the trees.

Now the parks are so quiet, it gives me a chill
to see no children outside and the swings hanging still.
There's no skipping or hopscotch, no church and no steeple,
we're a generation of idiots, smart phones and dumb people.

So look up from your phone, shut down that display,
take in your surroundings, and make the most of today.
Just one real connection is all it can take,
to show you the difference that being there can make.

Be there in the moment, when she gives you the look,
that you remember forever, as when love overtook.
The time you first hold her hand, or first kiss her lips,
the time you first disagree, but still love her to bits.

The time you don't need to tell hundreds, about what you've just done,
because you want to share the moment, with just this one.
The time you sell your computer, so you can buy a ring,
for the girl of your dreams, who is now the real thing.

The time you want to start a family, and the moment when,
you first hold your baby girl, and get to fall in love again.
The time she keeps you up at night, and all you want is rest,
and the time you wipe away the tears, as your baby flees the nest.

The time your little girl returns, with a boy for you to hold,
and the day he calls you granddad, and makes you feel real old
The time you take in all you've made, just by giving life attention,
and how your glad you didn't waste it, by looking down at some invention.

The time you hold your wife's hand, and sit down beside her bed
you tell her that you love her, and lay a kiss upon her head.
She then whispers to you quietly, as her heart gives a final beat,
that she's lucky she got stopped, by that lost boy in the street.

But none of these times ever happened, you never had any of this,
When you're too busy looking down, you don't see the chances you miss.

So look up from your phone, shut down those displays,
we have a finite existence, a set number of days.
Why waste all our time getting caught in the net,
as when the end comes, nothing's worse than regret.

I am guilty too, of being part of this machine,
this digital world, where we are heard but not seen.
Where we type and don't talk, where we read as we chat,
where we spend hours together, without making eye contact.

> Don't give in to a life where you follow the hype,
> give people your love, don't give them your like.
> Disconnect from the need to be heard and defined
> Go out into the world, leave distractions behind.
>
> Look up from your phone, shut down that display,
> stop watching this video, live life the real way.
> © http://garyturk.com/portfolio-item/lookup/

4 Solutions

A. Pre-viewing: possible answers

1. Are these really friends? – No, most of them are just names on the screen. – They don't really know each other.
2. Social media; they don't know each other in real life; »I speak to them« in the sense of »writing«.
3. They don't meet, don't talk to each other.
4. »Social« vs »doors we shut«: Even if you are connected to each other you are alone at home.

M 2

1. Loneliness, isolation, illusion, information gets sold, no emotions, no more real communication …
2. Back then, children played outside with friends; there were a lot of outdoor activities such as biking; »holes in trainers«, »graze up our knees« – Now the swings are hanging still; no skipping; no hopscotch
3. You can find a girl, fall in love, get married, get children, become granddad, love each other for a whole life
4. Don't give in to a life where you follow the hype,
Give people your love, don't give them your like.
Disconnect from the need to be heard and defined
Go out into the world, leave distractions behind.
Look up from your phone, shut down that display,
Stop watching this video, live life the real way.
5. The video poet intends viewers to reduce the amount of time spent on mobile phones and be open to real life instead.

Bibliography

Donaghy, Kieran (2015). Film in Action. Peaslake: Delta.
O'Neill, Megan (2011). »What makes a video ›viral‹?« *Social Times.* http://www.adweek.com/socialtimes/what-makes-a-video- viral / 62 414?red=st

Documentaries

Stefanie Rödel

1 Genre

The term *documentary* refers to a broad category of visual expression which is based on the attempt to document some aspect of reality, primarily in order to instruct, educate, or maintain a historical record (Grant / Sloniowski 1997). According to the Academy of Motion Picture Arts and Sciences (AMPAS), which awards the annual Oscars including the *Academy Award for Best Documentary (Short Subject)*, a short documentary film is a non-fiction motion picture with a run time of no more than 40 minutes dealing creatively with artistic, cultural, economic, historical, scientific, social, or other subjects (https://web.archive.org). It may be shot in actual occurrence, or can resort to partial re-enactment, stock footage, stills, animation, stop-motion or other techniques; the emphasis, however, must be on fact, not on fiction.

Short docus may treat various topics and employ different narration styles:

- Silent docu ▶ without words
- Voice-over narrator ▶ traditional style: invisible narrator reading a script dubbed onto the audio track
- Silent narration ▶ title screens visually narrating the documentary
- Hosted narrator ▶ a host appearing on camera, conducting interviews, also doing voice-overs

Apart from the annual Oscar nominations, several online platforms offer short documentaries worth watching. For example, UK based film studies lecturer Sarah Prokop has assembled a list of 20 short documentaries, which are not only of high artistic quality, but are also readily available to view online – from No. 20, *Employees Leaving the Lumière Factory*, a black-and-white silent documentary produced in 1895 by the celebrated Louis Lumière, to No. 3, *Talking Heads* (1980) by Polish film legend Krzysztof Kieslowski interviewing people from different ages, professions and social statuses, asking them all two questions (1. Who are you? 2. What do you want from life?), to No. 1, *Junkopia* (1981), a short experimental documentary by the late Chris Marker, which depicts strange inanimate objects contrasted with the contemporary world (www.tasteofcinema.com).

The type of short documentary film the following lesson plan is based on is a YouTube video on South Africa, which can be classified as a mixture of travel documentary and tourist agency commercial. The national authorities or tourist boards aim to make the viewers travel there, making use of the *AIDA-formula* (Thaler 2014: 75), i.e. to catch the viewers' attention, so that they become interested, feel a desire for the destination and finally travel there (Attention –Interest –Desire –Action).

2 Procedure

Title	Top 10 Amazing Facts About South Africa (09:05 min; www.youtube.com/watch?v=4_-SOlCGEik)
Synopsis	This country documentary presents and describes 10 outstanding aspects of South Africa: »Continuing our grand tour of the world, we're journeying back to the southern hemisphere to explore the highly suggested ... South Africa! From breathtaking waterfalls and majestic wildlife, to being home to some of the most intriguing shipwrecks to have ever been found, we'll take a look at 10 amazing facts about South Africa!« 10. Fame of South Africa 9. South African Innovations 8. South African Cuisine 7. Tourist Attractions 6. South African Wildlife 5. Increase in Education 4. South African Nature Attractions 3. Nuts over Mining and Minerals 2. A Land of Shipwrecks 1. The Cradle of Mankind
Competences	Listening-viewing, intercultural competence, speaking, writing, phonologic competence
Topics	Education, tourism, history, technology, culture
Level	Advanced
Time	45 minutes / 90 minutes

Steps: global-to-detail approach

1. Lead-in
a) T shows the beginning of the clip, freezes it, and has S describe it.
b) S try to anticipate the content of the video.
c) T writes the 10 facts (see above) in jumbled order on the board and asks S to put them into the right order while viewing (writing numbers down on a sheet of paper).
d) If necessary, T explains unknown key vocabulary.

2. First viewing (straight-through approach)
S watch the video clip in one sitting, and write down the numbers.

3. Global comprehension
a) The results are checked (correct order of scenes).
b) S add facts they can remember to each of the 10 facts.

4. Second viewing (segment approach)
a) A worksheet with questions on the 10 facts is distributed (M 1).
b) After each scene, the video is paused, and S take notes on the comprehension questions.

5. Detailed comprehension
a) The results are checked in pairs first.
b) For each scene, one S takes the role of the teacher and checks the answers in class.

6. Follow-up (Homework)
S can choose between three tasks:
a) Write a summary of the video in about 250 words.
b) Write an email to a friend of yours, giving him / her advice of what should be done and seen in South Africa.
c) Prepare a storyboard for a video on »10 Amazing Facts of ... (your home town)«.

3 Materials

M1: Worksheet

10 Amazing Facts about South Africa

Watch each scene separately and answer the questions below.

Scene 1: Fame of South Africa
1. Name at least 3 famous people coming from South Africa.
2. How long was Nelson Mandela President of South Africa?
3. What is Bishop Desmond Tutu famous for?
4. Are the following statements about Nelson Mandela correct, wrong or not in the clip?
a) Mandela was an anti-apartheid revolutionary politician and philanthropist.
b) He spent a long time in prison on Robben Island.
c) Later he was elected President of his home country.
d) Nelson Mandela is also called Morgan Freeman.

Scene 2: South African Innovations
5. What medical device was invented by Allan McLeod Cormack?
6. What is »Pratley Patty«, and what was it used for?
7. What are the geometric blocks used for?
8. Name two other South African innovations.

Scene 3: South African Cuisine
9. What are »Koeksisters«?
10. Which of these dishes is not special for South Africa: Bobotie – Potjiekos – French Fries – Frikadelle – Biltong – Beef Jerky – Roasted Butternut?
11. What is special about South African cuisine?
12. Can you recommend a South African restaurant? Why is it special?

Scene 4: Tourist Attractions
13. Where can you go if you are interested in the history of South Africa?
14. What site is specific for the gold rush in South Africa?
15. What city is famous for its beautiful beaches?
16. Name at least three other sites and places that are famous in South Africa.

Scene 5: Wildlife
17. What are the Big Five.
18. Name three animals that can be detected around the Cape region especially.
19. How many mammals in South Africa are (critically) endangered?
20. What animals live in South Africa that one would not expect to be there? Where can you see them?

Scene 6: Increase in Education
21. What has changed in terms of education in South Africa?

Scene 7: South African Nature Attractions
22. How old are Makhonjwa Mountains, and where are they located?
23. What is special about the Tugela Falls?
24. What is the largest green canyon called?

Scene 8: Mining and Nuts
25. What natural products are mined in South Africa?
26. What is the value of the greatest remaining diamond reserve?
27. What is special about South Africa and the Macadamia Nut?

Scene 9: Shipwrecks
28. Name three ships that sank around the shore of Cape Town.
29. What were the reasons for the accidents?

30. What innovation did the accidents lead to?
31. According to the legend, who or what did the sailors see?

Scene 10: Cradle of Mankind
32. What has been discovered in the Cradle of Mankind in general?
33. What famous discovery was made in 1947?

4 Solutions

M1: Answers to worksheet
1. Nelson Mandela, Desmond Tutu, Charlize Theron, J.R.R Tolkien
2. Five years
3. He is famous for winning the Nobel Peace Prize.
4. Correct / not in the clip / correct / wrong
5. The transverse axial scanning / CAT scan
6. It is an adhesive, and it was used at the Apollo XI moon landing.
7. Protecting harbour walls
8. Solar cells, speed gun
9. Sweet, deep-fried pastries, eaten for desert
10. French Fries, Beef Jerky
11. It is a mixture of indigenous flavours and influences from colonists (German, French, Italian, British and Greek).
12. The Gold Restaurant in Cape Town: drumming session, customary hand-washing ceremony
13. District Six Museum
14. The Big Hole in Kimberly
15. Cape Town
16. Kruger National Park, uShaka Marine World, West Coast Fossil Park, Cradle of Humankind, South African National Museum of Military History
17. Elephant, buffalo, lion, rhino, leopard
18. Cape horseshoe bat, geometric tortoise, southern adder, cape legless shink, blue crane, mountain zebra, blue whale
19. 13 endangered and critically endangered mammals
20. Penguins at Boulders Beach
21. changes in education:

- 4 % increase of people aged 20 and older who obtained some type of higher education
- Number of people with no schooling at all dropped
- Illiteracy rates dropped from 31.5 % to 19.1 % in one decade

22. 3.6 billion years old, located along the border of Mpumalanga and Swaziland
23. It is the 2nd tallest waterfall in the world.
24. Blyde River Canyon
25. Manganese, chrome, diamonds, vanadium, gold
26. $ 2.5 trillion
27. South Africa is the leading export country for macadamia nuts with 25 % of the world supply in 2014.
28. Sacramento, Grosvenor, Waratah, Arniston
29. The reefs were very dangerous and hardly visible.
30. It led to the construction of lighthouses.
31. The Flying Dutchman
32. 40 % of all human ancestor fossils have been discovered in South Africa.
33. 1947: discovery of the Australopithecus africanus

Bibliography

Grant, Barry / Sloniowski, Jeannette (eds.). 1997. Documenting the Documentary: Close Readings of Documentary Film and Video. Detroit: Wayne State University Press.
Thaler, Engelbert (2014). Teaching English with Films. Paderborn: Schöningh.
www.tasteofcinema.com/2014/20-of-the-best-documentary-shorts-you-can-watch-online/2/#ixzz4UsbhZD00. https://web.archive.org/web/20150226053423/http://www.oscars.org:80/sites/default/files/88aa_rule11_doc_short.pdf.

Weather Forecasts

Angelika Pfeil

1 Genre

»Everybody talks about the weather« (James 1986: 95). Weather reports are part of authentic non-fiction videos, programmes about real life, and familiar formats, which are close to the students' lives and address matters of common interest (Sherman 2003: 60). Working with weather reports, you equip students with the necessary vocabulary and understanding you need in order to participate in everyday conversation.

However, due to the fast speech rate, weather reports pose certain comprehension problems. These can be compensated if instructors »prepare video materials carefully [...] [and choose] tasks [...] [which are] tailored to the students' abilities« (Lutcavage 1992: 33). In particular, pre-viewing activities seem crucial for the students' understanding of the weather report (Lutcavage 1992: 36 f.), for example »conducting a brainstorming session with the class [or] [...] using a newspaper weather report as a means of familiarizing the students with appropriate terminology«. Additionally the telling weather symbols can act as supporting devices. Lutcavage (Ib.) also advises teachers to foster intercultural knowledge and skills by addressing the different temperature scales of Celsius and Fahrenheit or by discussing the differences between American / British and German weather forecasts in general.

2 Procedure

Lesson A (LOWER GRADES)

Title	Dundee Weather Report for Kids (https://www.youtube.com/watch?v=rh-4Orzh-p4)
Synopsis	Two young adults describe the weather for Dundee, Scotland, for Monday, Tuesday, Wednesday and Thursday, and give recommendations on what to wear and do on these days.
Competences	Viewing, listening-viewing, (creative) writing, speaking, listening, lexical competence

Topics	Weather, weather forecast, clothes, activities, directions, UK, Republic of Ireland
Level	Beginners
Time	45 minutes

Steps (PWP approach):

A. Pre-viewing
1. T: »Look out of the window! What's the weather like today?«
2. T: »When you talk about the weather, it's very helpful to know the different directions. Who can help me to write down the eight directions of this compass?« (M 1)

B. While-viewing
1. First viewing (sound off): T plays the video and asks S to fill in the worksheet (M 2) as far as possible while watching the weather forecast.
2. Second viewing (with sound): T plays the clip a second time, so S can check their first guesses.
3. Worksheet (M 2) is corrected, and S can ask about unknown expressions (windproof, to fly a kite, earmuffs ...).

C. Post-viewing
Role play: S work together in pairs on worksheets M 3 and M 4. While partner A is describing the weather on the map (M 3), partner B is listening and completing the blank map (M 4) with his / her own drawings of weather symbols. Afterwards, they compare their maps / solutions.

Homework: creative writing
Write an email to an English friend who wants to visit you and tell him what activities you can do in your hometown when it is raining / snowing / the sun is shining etc. Write at least about five different activities. The worksheet (M 2) will help you.

Lesson B (HIGHER GRADES)

Title	BBC Weather, 1 July 2015, UK Forecast (https://www.youtube.com/watch?v=HY3Y3IyK6vk)
Synopsis	The BBC weather presenter informs about the weather in the UK from Wednesday, 1 July 2015, to Friday, 5 July 2015 (2 minutes 29 seconds).
Competences	Listening-viewing, lexical competence, speaking, method competence (presentations), creative writing
Topics	Weather, weather forecast, UK

Level	Intermediate
Time	45 minutes

Steps (PWP approach)

A. Pre-viewing
1. T states »I always feel happy when the snow is falling in June«, and waits for the S to react.
2. Vocabulary: Ideas and lexemes concerning the word field »weather« are collected on the blackboard in the form of a mind map.

B. While-viewing
1. First viewing: T plays the video and asks S afterwards what they can remember.
2. Worksheet (M 1) is handed out and read so that S know what to focus on.
3. Second viewing
4. S fill in the exercise.
5. The results are discussed, and unknown expressions (flooding issues, peak, humidity, average …) are explained.

C. Post-viewing
We, the meteorologists:
1. In groups of three, S are asked to prepare their own weather forecast with the help of a map of the UK (M 2) and weather symbols (M 3). They are expected to use at least three expressions from the worksheet (M 1) and an appropriate greeting (e.g. »Hello there!«). Variations of the phrases from the worksheet are also possible (e.g. »temperatures in the low thirties«).
2. Some groups present their weather forecast to the class. With the help of a document camera, the presenters make use of the map (M 2) and the weather symbols (M 3) to illustrate their predictions. The rest of the class must find out which phrases from the worksheet (M 1) were used.

Homework: creative writing
Observe the weather in your hometown very closely for the next four days and write your own weather report about it. Use as many different expressions as possible. The worksheet (M 1) will help you.

3 Materials

Lesson A

M 1: Compass (http://360investmentadvice.com/wp-content/uploads/2012/12/HiRes.jpg, adapted)

M 2: Dundee weather forecast

Dundee Weather Report Watch the video and fill in the table.			
	Weather	Clothes	Activities
Monday			
Tuesday			
Wednesday			
Thursday			

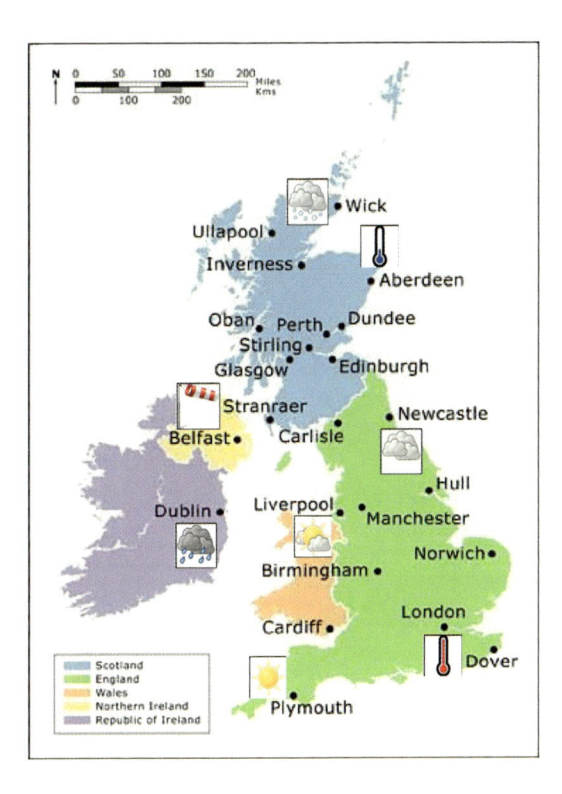

M 3: Map A (Partner A) (www.willkommeninschottland.com/reise/nach-schottland-kommen/entfernungen-zwischen-schottisch, adapted)

M 4: Map B (Partner B) (www.willkommeninschottland.com/reise/nach-schottland-kommen/entfernungen-zwischen-schottisch, adapted)

Lesson B

M1: Weather Bingo

> **BBC Weather: 1 July 2015 UK Forecast**
> *Which chunks did you hear? Tick the correct boxes. NB: The phrases are not in the correct order.*
> - Heavy showers and even some thunderstorms
> - There's a hurricane warning
> - High humidity levels
> - Brighten up with some sunshine
> - Localized flooding issues
> - A fresh wind is blowing

- Temperatures up in the high twenties
- Minimum temperatures overnight
- Our heatwave has reached its peak
- An average temperature of 24 degrees
- The sun is burning down in the south-east of England
- Temperatures have dropped off
- Into the weekend, it's a mixed affair

M 2: Map of the UK (http://static.bbci.co.uk/weather/0.5.382/images/coast-and-sea/tide-table-maps/0.png)

M 3: Weather symbols (http://cliparts.co/cliparts/pcq/K5M/pcqK5MBni.png, adapted)

4 Solutions

Lesson A

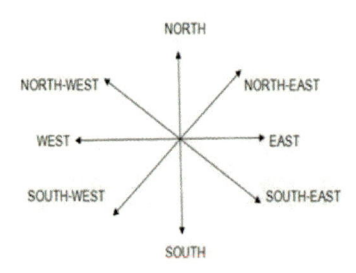

M 1: Weather directions

	Weather	Clothes	Activities
Monday	rain / it's raining, clouds / cloudy	rain jacket, umbrella	stay inside and watch a film
Tuesday	wind / windy, clouds / cloudy	windproof coat, no umbrella	flying a kite
Wednesday	snowy / it's snowing, sunny / the sun is shining	warm coat, earmuffs	make a snowman
Thursday	sunny / the sun is shining, hot	T-shirt, sunglasses	good day for the beach

M 2: Dundee weather forecast

M 3: Partner A's weather report

- The sun is shining / It's sunny in the south-west of England / in Plymouth.
- It's hot in the south of England / in London and Dover.
- In the north of Wales, it's cloudy and / but sunny / the sun is shining.
- It's cloudy / There are many clouds in the north-east of England / in Newcastle.
- It's very windy / stormy in Northern Ireland / in Belfast.
- It's raining / rainy in the south-east of the Republic of Ireland / in Dublin.
- It's very cold in the east of Scotland / in Aberdeen.
- In the (very) north of Scotland / In Wick, it's snowing / snowy.

Lesson B

A. 1. Possible student reactions:

- »Are you kidding / pulling our legs?«
- »My mood isn't dependent on the weather. I'm either happy or sad, but that's not linked to the weather.«
- »I totally agree. When the sun is shining, I always feel happier, even if something bad has happened.«
- »Sometimes, that's true. But I'm not always happy when the sun is shining. And I'm not always sad when it's raining.«

A. 2. Possible words for the mind map with the word »weather« in the middle:
good, bad, hot, dry, warm, bright, cold, cool, fresh, sun, sunny, sunshine, clouds, cloudless, cloudy, wind, windy, snow, snowy, rain, rainy, storm, stormy,

(minimum / maximum) temperature, degree, natural catastrophe, tornado, thunderstorm, seasons, summer, spring, autumn / fall, winter ...

M 1: Weather Bingo
Correct phrases: Heavy showers and even some thunderstorms / Brighten up with some sunshine / Localized flooding issues / Temperatures up in the high twenties / Minimum temperatures overnight / Our heatwave has reached its peak / Temperatures have dropped off / Into the weekend, it's a mixed affair

Bibliography

James, Charles. »Doing Something about the Weather.« Die Unterrichtspraxis / Teaching German 19.1 (1986): 95–101.

Lutcavage, Charles. »Authentic Video in Intermediate German.« Die Unterrichtspraxis / Teaching German 25.1 (1992): 33–40.

Sherman, Jane. Using Authentic Video in the Language Classroom. Cambridge: Cambridge University Press, 2003.

Contributors

Prof. Dr. Gabriele Blell

Gabriele Blell is full Professor of TEFL at the Leibniz University of Hannover. She studied English and Russian at the University of Potsdam, Germany. After her studies she worked at a grammar school for several years before continuing her academic career in Potsdam and Hannover.

Her main research interests include inter-/transcultural learning, teaching with literature and films, media and digital literacy, cross-linked learning (English and Spanish), teacher education, as well as Blended and Mobile Learning. Her recent publications include *Web 2.0 und komplexe Kompetenzaufgaben im FSU* (eds. Becker, Blell, Rössler) (2016) and *Film in den Fächern der sprachlichen Bildung* (eds. Blell, Grünewald, Kepser and Surkamp) (2016). She is also co-editor of the book series *Foreign Language Pedagogy – content- and learner-oriented* (eds. Becker, Blell, Kupetz).

Prof. Dr. Matthias Hutz

Matthias Hutz is a Professor of Applied Linguistics and English Language Teaching at Freiburg University of Education. His doctoral thesis was entitled *Kontrastive Fachtextlinguistik für den fachbezogenen Fremdsprachenunterricht*, and he also published a pedagogical grammar for students of English. He worked at the Universities of Giessen, Madison (Wisconsin/USA), Heidelberg and Wuppertal.

His main research interests include the study of second-language acquisition, bilingual education, text linguistics, English for Specific Purposes (ESP), and intercultural learning. His current research focuses on language immersion, contrastive pragmatics and the teaching of lexico-grammar. He has also been involved in several EU-funded projects in Teaching English as a Foreign Language in Eastern Europe.

Prof. Dr. Christiane Lütge

Christiane Lütge holds the Chair for Teaching English as a Foreign Language (TEFL) at the University of Munich (LMU). Areas of interest include media and film literacy, transcultural learning and global education, literature in the EFL classroom and the impact of digital culture on foreign language learning. She has published widely on various aspects of foreign language teacher education and is a co-editor of the international online journal on children's literature (clelejournal.org) as well as a co-editor of Praxis Fremdsprachenunterricht.

Prof. Dr. Klaus Maiwald

Klaus Maiwald is full Professor of Didactics of German Language and Literature at Augsburg University. After studying English and German at Würzburg University and the Univ. of Georgia (M. A. in English/American Literature), he taught Gymnasium for several years. Maiwald did his Ph. D. and his post-doctoral work (habilitation) at Bamberg University. Among his research interests are teaching literature (esp. literature for children and young adults) and film. His most recent book publication is *Vom Film zur Literatur. Moderne Klassiker der Literaturverfilmung im Medienvergleich* (2015).

Genia Markova

Genia Markova teaches English, Technical English and French at an automotive vocational school in Berlin. She also works as a translator from German to Russian at DPA (German Press Agency). She writes poetry, has been a poetry slam artist since 2008, having won numerous slam battles in Hamburg, Nuremberg and Berlin. She organizes Russian poetry slams in Berlin and introduced the first annual Russian Women poetry slam in 2014, in order to promote female artists. She is one of the organizers of the multicultural festival *RuBERoid*. Markova is also an editor of the Russian literary magazine *Berlin. Berega*.

Prof. Dr. Annika McPherson

Annika McPherson is Juniorprofessor for New English Literatures and Cultural Studies at the University of Augsburg. She previously taught British and Global Anglophone Literary and Cultural Studies at Carl von Ossietzky University Oldenburg. Her research and teaching areas include postcolonial studies; theories, policies and literary representations of cultural diversity in comparative perspective; Caribbean, West African, South African and Indian literatures in English; diaspora studies; as well as speculative fiction and Afrofuturism. Her monograph "White-Female-Postcolonial? Towards a 'Trans-cultural Reading of Marina Warner's Indigo and Barbara Kingsolver's The Poisonwood Bible" was published in 2011. Her most recent articles focus on postcolonial and decolonial critique and Afropolitan aesthetics. Her current book projects include a study of the representation of Rastafari in literature and film, a genre critique of the notion of 'neo-slave narratives', as well as a co-edited collection on "Practices of Resistance: Narratives, Politics, and Aesthetics across the Caribbean and Its Diasporas."

Jana Pessozki

Jana Pessozki teaches English and Russian at Friedensburg Oberschule in Berlin. Her key interests in teaching foreign languages are the use of modern media, the development of intercultural competence and film literacy. She is a coordinator of the project *Notebook classes* at her school and is a teacher consultant for English language at *ProSchul* (Berlin Ministry of Education, Youth and Family Affairs).

She has published about 40 contributions to the journal *Praxis Fremdsprachenunterricht* and is also author of several Russian language coursebooks. She sat at the same school desk with Genia Markova, the co-author of the article printed in this book; this happened long ago in Ukraine where her love for the English language and the dream to be an English teacher were born.

Prof. Dr. Engelbert Thaler

Engelbert Thaler is full Professor of TEFL at Augsburg University. After teaching English at Gymnasium for 20 years, he did his doctoral thesis on *Musikvideoclips im Englischunterricht* and his habilitation at Ludwig-Maximilians-Universität, Munich on *Offene Lernarrangements im Englischunterricht. Rekonstruktion, Konstruktion, Konzeption, Exemplifikation, Integration.*

His research foci are improving teaching quality *(Balanced Teaching)*, teacher education and training, developing coursebooks, media literacy, and teaching literature. He has published more than 550 contributions to TEFL. His recent publications include *Englisch unterrichten, Shorties – Flash Fiction in Language Teaching,* and *Standard-basierter Englischunterricht.* Thaler is also editor of the journal *Praxis Fremdsprachenunterricht* and of several coursebooks.

Christoph Werth

Christoph Werth currently teaches English and French as foreign languages at Gymnasium Wertingen near Augsburg. After his final exams at the University of Augsburg and in Regensburg, the State of Bavaria has taken him in as a fulltime member of staff right away.

Moreover, since 2012, Christoph Werth has been active as a lecturer for the Chair of English Didactics at the University of Augsburg. In his courses, Mr Werth focuses on giving future generations of teachers a realistic glimpse at their future practice. Lastly, Mr Werth has been awarded the Deutsche Lehrerpreis in 2012, a prize for teachers of nation-wide reputation in Germany – his own pupils had recommended him to the committee.